すぐ使える **英文** テーマ別
**ライティングの
エッセンス**

小林兼之／ガリー・ハント ── 共著

Copyright © Kaneyuki Kobayashi and Gary Hunt, 2004

All rights reserved, including the right to reproduce this book or portions thereof in any form.

First edition: September 2004

Published by Kenkyusha Ltd.

Printed in Japan by Kenkyusha Printing Co.

本 書 の 利 用 法

　英文を書く演習をより効果的に，より実際的にするため，本書は文法事項を二次的なものとし，テーマ別の構成を主軸としている．したがって，本書は必ずしも第1章から読み始めなくてもよい．読者の皆さんが興味をもち，好きなテーマがあれば，そこからスタートすればいい．例えば，スポーツに熱中していたら，第8章から，英会話の実力を向上させたいと望むなら，第10章，手紙文なら第6章などと，それぞれ自由に始めるのが得策である．そのため，各章の語句・例文の下に与えられている文法事項の説明は，どの章から読んでも，何の困難，支障もなく理解できるよう最大の注意が払われている．

　各章の構成は，Check & Check ⇨ Let's Try ⇨ Let's Memorize ⇨ Exercises の4つの部分から成っている．

　Check & Check は，本書の主要部分で，英字新聞や雑誌などに頻出し，しかも慣用表現として重要と思われる語句や短文を収集した．▶印は，和文を英訳する観点から注目すべき文法事項の補足説明，書き換え，同意・反意表現などを示す．なお，本文中の [　] は，置換可能語句，同意・類似表現を，(　) は，省略可能を表わす．

　Let's Try は，Check & Check の学習後，その習熟度を確認するために設けたもので，問題の8割までは復習用である．もし問題中に不明のところがあった場合は，再三再四，Check & Check を調べ，再挑戦することを望む．「解答」を見る前に，ぜひとも Check & Check を反復練習して欲しい．この反復学習こそ，英文ライティングの秘訣である．

Let's Memorize に与えられている模範例文は，やさしい語句と構文を用い，日常話されているスタイルにしてある．和文と英文を左右対照にし，日本語と英語の間に見られる発想の違いが容易に理解できるようにしてある．これらの模範例文を完全に，正確に暗記するように努めれば，必ず口語英語をマスターする一助となろう．正確に記憶する方法として，ノートなどに模範英文を書き写し，繰り返し音読することをすすめたい．

Exercises は，新聞・雑誌などの記事から，既習の語句や構文を使って書ける内容のものを，各章5問前後精選した．各問題には，[語句]，[考え方]を与え，各自が自分の英語力で，少しでも容易に解答できるヒントになるよう工夫した．そのため，〈解答例〉を見る前に，まず[語句]，[考え方]を参考にして，ノートなどに**自分の英文を書くこと**を期待する．自分の英文が，たとえ〈解答例〉とどんなに異なっていても，落胆することはない．〈解答例〉は2通り与えられている．(**i**) は，比較的やさしい語句や基本的構文を用いたもの，(**ii**) は，やや高度な構文で，より自然なスタイルのものである．

以上4つの構成中，Check & Check と Let's Try と Let's Memorize の3つの部分は，いつでも，どこでも学習できる部分である．通勤通学の途上の車中でも，散歩中でも，どんな短い時間の休憩中でも，同じページを何回となく反復して学習を継続すれば，英文のリズムが会得され，表現力がますます向上するだろう．また，重要と思われるところにマーカーなどを用いてアンダーライン等を引くのも記憶を助ける方法である．

小 林 兼 之

＊本書は『英作文にすぐ使える　頻出語句・例文集』として出版されていたものを，皆様からのご要望に応える形でサイズを拡大し，内容を一部変更してリニューアルした新装改訂版です．

目　　次

本書の利用法 iii

第 1 章　　天候・季節 . . . .　1

第 2 章　　衣・食・住 17

第 3 章　　健康・病気 31

第 4 章　　人生・生活・時間 45

第 5 章　　交通・旅行 62

第 6 章　　社交・通信 78

第 7 章　　風俗・習慣 94

第 8 章　　趣味・娯楽・運動 110

第 9 章　　天災・災難・事故 127

第 10 章　　読書・語学 143

第11章	文化・芸術・科学	160
第12章	教育・勉強・学校	176
第13章	政治・経済・産業	193
第14章	道徳・思想・感情	210
第15章	社会・環境・国際事情	226
Index		243

第 1 章
天候・季節

Check & Check

☐ 今年の冬は好天に恵まれている ⇨ We have been having good weather this winter.
  ▶このweatherには good, bad などの形容詞をつけることができ，無冠詞

☐ その日は上天気になりました ⇨ It turned out to be a beautiful [wonderful, lovely] day.
  ▶It is fine today. よりも，The weather is nice [good] today. とか，It's a nice day today. などというのが普通

☐ 山の天気は変わりやすい ⇨ The weather in the mountains changes easily.
  ▶weather が主語として文頭に置かれたときには the を伴う

☐ 晴れた日には富士山が見える ⇨ In clear weather we can

see Mt. Fuji.
▶この句では，weather に冠詞を用いない．On a clear day …といってもよい

□天気予報によれば ⇨ according to the weather forecast
▶同意語句として，The weather forecast [report] says… とか The weatherman says… も用いられる

□天気がよければ ⇨ weather permitting
▶無冠詞で文尾によく用いられる

□晴雨(せいう)にかかわらず ⇨ rain or shine
▶whatever the weather is like ともいう

□天気が続くでしょう ⇨ I hope the weather will stay fine.
▶この weather は「その日その日の天気模様」をさす

□天気がぐずついている ⇨ The weather is unsettled.

□この気候は君の体に適しているようです ⇨ This weather seems to agree with you.

□空模様が怪しい ⇨ The sky is threatening.
▶The sky の代わりに The weather も用いられる

□晴れそうだ ⇨ It's going to clear up.

□雨が降りそうだ ⇨ It looks like rain.

□雨が降ったりやんだりしている ⇨ It is raining on and off [off and on].

□昨日，にわか雨にあい，ずぶぬれだ ⇨ Yesterday I was caught in a shower and got wet [drenched, soaked] to the skin.
▶meet a shower とはいわない．「雨にあった」は I was caught in *the* rain．となる．冠詞に注意

□今朝はひどいどしゃ降りだ ⇨ It's really pouring this

morning.
　▶It's raining cats and dogs. はやや古い同意表現
□しとしと雨が降っている ⇒ It's drizzling.
　▶「こぬか雨」は a fine rain ともいう
□雨はいつあがるだろう ⇒ When will the rain let up?
　▶let up の代わりに, stop も用いられる. なお, 動詞表現で, When will it stop raining? ともいう
□午後ところにより, にわか雨になるだろう ⇒ Scattered showers are expected this afternoon.
　▶We を主語にして, We'll have scattered showers in the afternoon. もよい. *cf.*「シャワーを浴びる」は have [take] *a* shower と不定冠詞をつけて使う
□この空模様では ⇒ from the look of the sky
□久しく雨がないですね ⇒ It has not rained for a long time.
　▶It has not been raining ～ は誤り. We を主語にして, We have been without rain for a long time. も同意表現
□日照り続き ⇒ a long spell of dry weather
　▶単に a long dry spell ともいう.「去年の今ごろは日照り続きでした」は, We had a dry spell about this time last year. となる
□この夏は雨が多[少な]かった ⇒ We have had a lot of [little] rain this summer.
□雨がやんだ ⇒ The rain is over.
　▶動詞表現にすると, It has stopped raining. となる
□木の下で雨やどりした ⇒ I took shelter from the rain under the tree.
　▶「避難する」の意では take refuge も用いられ, 通例, 無

冠詞

☐雨はもうたくさんだ ⇨ We have had enough of rain.

☐かさを持ってくればよかったと思う ⇨ I wish I had brought my umbrella with me.

☐暖かい[厳しい]冬 ⇨ a mild [severe] winter
　▶「去年は暖冬だった」⇨ We had a mild winter last year. この表現では，不定冠詞 a と mild, severe などの形容詞をつける

☐夕方ごろ雨が雪に変わってきた ⇨ Toward evening the rain changed to snow.

☐雪は冬のたよりだ ⇨ Snow indicates the coming of winter.

☐東京では昨夜雪が降った ⇨ We had snow in Tokyo last night.
　▶動詞表現で，It snowed in Tokyo last night. ともいえる

☐昨夜大雪が降った ⇨ A lot of snow fell last night.
　▶この snow は不可算名詞. 動詞表現は，It snowed a lot [heavily] last night. となる

☐10年ぶりの大雪だ ⇨ This is the heaviest snowfall in ten years.

☐真冬に ⇨ in the depths [dead] of winter
　▶「真夏に」⇨ in the height of summer

☐今年は例年に比べて雪が少ない ⇨ This year we have had [there has been] less snow than usual.

☐このへんはよく雪が降る ⇨ We have frequent snowfalls in this part of the country.

第1章　天候・季節

- □日の当たるところは雪がすぐ解ける ⇨ The snow soon melts in the sun.
- □この地方は深刻な水不足になるだろう ⇨ There will be a serious shortage of water in this area.
  - ▶形容詞表現にすると，This area will run short of water. となる
- □日本の気候は春が一番よい ⇨ The climate of Japan is most delightful in spring.
  - ▶climate は「ある土地特有の平均気候」をいい，一定の土地では長期にわたった状況に変化がない
- □英国の気候をどうお思いですか ⇨ How do you like [find] the climate of England?
- □今年は春のくるのが遅い ⇨ The spring is late in coming this year.
  - ▶口語では in が省略される
- □日ごとに暖かくなってきた ⇨ It is getting warmer day by day.
- □初春に ⇨ early in spring / in early spring
- □だんだんどこも春めいてきた ⇨ It is getting springlike everywhere.
- □春のきざし ⇨ a sign of spring
- □若葉が萌(も)え始めた ⇨ The fresh young leaves have come out.
- □4月にしては少々寒い ⇨ It is rather [a little] cold for April.
- □庭のバラが咲いている ⇨ The roses are blooming in my garden.

□当地の桜は4月の初めに満開だろう ⇨ The cherry blossoms here will be at their best at the beginning of April.
　▶同意表現：The cherry trees here will be in full bloom at the beginning of April.

□梅雨にはいった[が明けた] ⇨ The rainy season has set in [is over].
　▶日本のような梅雨がない国では，雨の多い季節のことを a wet spell という

□当地は6月はいつも雨が多い ⇨ Rainy weather is the rule here in June.
　▶動詞表現：It usually rains a lot here in June.

□今ごろは湿度が高い ⇨ Humidity is high at this time of the year.
　▶形容詞表現：It's very humid at this time of the year.

□我慢できない蒸し暑さだ ⇨ It is unbearably sultry.

□雲が地平線に低くたれこめている ⇨ The clouds are hanging low on the horizon.
　▶「雲」の意味のときは複数形 clouds が普通

□夏は冬よりも日の出がずっと早い ⇨ In summer the sun rises much earlier than in winter.

□夏は日が長い ⇨ In summer the days are long.
　▶この意味では，「日」は複数形．*cf.*「夜が明けないうちに出かけよう」は，Let's leave before *day* breaks. day の単数，無冠詞に注意

□濃霧 ⇨ a dense [thick, heavy] fog

□船が間もなく霧の中に見えなくなった ⇨ The boat was soon lost sight of in the fog.

第1章　天候・季節

□霧が晴れた ⇨ The fog cleared [lifted].

□北風が吹いていた ⇨ The wind was blowing from the north.
　▶この The wind の代わりに It も用いられる．全文を There was a north wind blowing. とすることもできる

□今日は雷がありそうだ ⇨ We're going to have thunder today.
　▶動詞表現：It's going to thunder today.

□雷が鳴ると，うちの子は食卓の下にかくれる ⇨ My child always hides under the table when it thunders.

□学校の夏休みはいつからですか ⇨ When will your school break up for the summer?
　▶the summer は「その年の夏」の意

□避暑[寒]に〜へ行く ⇨ go to 〜 for the summer [winter]

□避暑[寒]地 ⇨ a summer [winter] resort
　▶この resort は「保養地」の意で，a mountain [seaside] resort などという．cf.「観光地」a tourist spot

□暑いのは平気だ ⇨ I don't mind the heat.
　▶「暑くてやりきれない」⇨ I can't stand the heat.

□台風の季節 ⇨ the typhoon season

□その台風は九州の南端に接近しつつある ⇨ The typhoon is approaching the southern tip of Kyushu.
　▶この approach は他動詞で，to を伴わない．台風を，日本では「台風11号」などと番号で呼ぶが，アメリカでは Kitty, Catherine などと人名などで呼ぶ

□カキは今が旬(しゅん)です ⇨ Oysters are now in season.
　▶「季節はずれ」⇨ out of season. この表現では無冠詞

□伊豆の温泉場は，この秋，近年にないにぎわいであった ⇨ The hot-springs in Izu this autumn have had the busiest season in years.
　▶この表現では，season に定冠詞 the と形容詞をつける

□初[晩]秋 ⇨ early [late] in autumn / in early [late] autumn

□豊[不]作 ⇨ a rich [poor] crop

□秋は暑すぎず，寒すぎず，読書に最もよい季節です ⇨ In autumn it is neither too hot nor too cold; it is the best season for reading.

□温度の激変 ⇨ a sudden change in the temperature

□温度が上がる[下がる] ⇨ The temperature rises [falls].

□現在の気温は摂氏15度です ⇨ The temperature reads [registers, stands at] 15 degrees C.
　▶The temperature の代わりに，The thermometer も用いられる．C は Centigrade または Celsius の略．欧米では，華氏 (Fahrenheit), 略して F で温度をいうのが普通

□コートを着ないと寒い ⇨ I feel chilly without a coat.
　▶寒さにふるえる ⇨ shiver with cold

□今朝はひどく霜がおりた ⇨ We had a severe [heavy] frost this morning.
　▶形容詞がつかないと，frost は無冠詞．Frost falls. のようにいう

□紅葉の名所 ⇨ a place noted for its autumn-tinted leaves
　▶「紅葉する」⇨ The leaves turn red [brown].

□雪が5センチ積っている ⇨ The snow lies five centimeters deep on the ground.

□雪道 ⇨ a snow-covered road *cf.* 雪嶺 ⇨ a snow-capped

mountain
▶雪合戦をする ⇨ have a snowball fight / 雪ダルマを作る ⇨ make a snowman

□雪国 ⇨ the snowy parts of the country
▶snow country とはいわない

□この冬は例年にない寒さだった ⇨ This winter has been severer than usual.
▶It を主語にし，It has been unusually cold this winter. ともいえる

Let's Try

【I】 次の各組の英文が同じような意味になるように，(b) の空所に適語を入れなさい．
1. (a) It looks like rain.
   (b) It seems as if (　　) is going to rain.
2. (a) According to the weather report, we will have showers today.
   (b) The weatherman (　　) showers today.
3. (a) When the weather is good, cycling is a lot of fun.
   (b) Whether cycling is enjoyable (　　) upon the weather.
4. (a) Whatever the weather is like, I will go out tomorrow.
   (b) Rain or (　　), I will go out tomorrow.
5. (a) It has rained for three days without stopping.
   (b) It has rained for three days without (　　) up.

6. (a) The mountain air does me good.
   (b) The mountain air (　　) with me.
7. (a) I hope the weather will improve tomorrow.
   (b) I hope the weather will (　　) up tomorrow.
8. (a) It is raining very heavily.
   (b) It is raining cats and (　　).
9. (a) It has not rained for a month.
   (b) We have had a dry (　　) for a month.
10. (a) We have never had such a heavy snowfall.
    (b) This is the (　　) snowfall we have ever had.

■[考え方] 1.天候を指す代名詞. 2.「予報する」 3.「～いかんによる」 4.「晴雨にかかわらず」 5.「やむことなく」 6.「適する」 7.「晴れる」 8.「どしゃ降り」 9.「期間」 10. heavy の最上級

■[解答] 1. it 2. predicts [forecasts] 3. depends 4. shine 5. letting 6. agrees 7. clear 8. dogs 9. spell 10. heaviest

【II】 つぎの各英文が，それぞれ下の和文に相当するように，(　　) 内に適当な1語を補いなさい.
1. The river is (　　) after yesterday's rain.
   (昨日の雨で川が増水している)
2. The weather has changed (　　) the better.
   (天気がもち直した)
3. The scenery changes (　　) the season.
   (季節によって景色が変わる)
4. The weather shows no (　　) of change.
   (天気が変わる気配がない)

5. The roses in the garden have come into (   ).
（庭のバラが咲いた）

■[考え方]　1. rise の進行形　2. 方向の前置詞　3. 同時進行の前置詞　4.「徴候」　5.「開花」
■[解　答]　1. rising　2. for　3. with　4. sign　5. bloom [flower]

Let's Memorize

1. 明日はどんな天気になるだろう．	What will the weather be like tomorrow?
2. 夕焼けがきれいだから，明日はたいてい晴れるよ．	With this pretty sunset, it will probably be a nice day tomorrow.
3. 今日はお天気で良かったね．	I'm glad the weather is nice today.
4. 春になって，山の雪が解け始めた．	In spring, the snow on the mountains began to thaw.
5. 今年の梅雨は去年に比べて雨が少ない．	This year's rainy season has been dry compared with last year's.
6. 天気予報で，今年は冷夏だといっていた．	The weather report says we are going to have [it is going to be] a cool summer this year.
7. 天気はまだぐずついているようです．	The weather still looks unsettled.
8. ずいぶんお天気が続いていますね．	We are having a long spell of agreeable weather.

9. そろそろひと雨ほしい頃ですね. | It's about time we had rain.

10. 風で彼女の帽子が飛ばされた. | The wind has blown her hat off.

11. 夏は夜が明けるのが早い. | Day breaks early in summer.

12. 秋は夜になると急に寒くなります. | In fall it turns cold suddenly at nightfall.

13. 東京地方の天気は今夜から下り坂になるでしょう. | The weather in the Tokyo area will take a turn for the worse tonight.

14. 「こんないい天気にどうしてかさを持っているの」「だって, 天気予報で降るっていったんだ」 | "Why are you carrying an umbrella around on a nice day like this?" "Well, the weather forecast said it is supposed to rain."

15. 農産物の生産高は天候に左右されることが多い. | Agricultural output is often affected by the weather.

Exercises

〈例題 1〉
3月10日には当地では寒暖計が25度を指し, まるで夏がきたような暑さでした.

■[語句]「3月10日」the tenth of March. これを略して, March 10th としてもよい
■[考え方]「...度を指す」は, stand at, read または show のいずれでもよいが, この場合は「...度に上がる」と考え, rise to や go up to とすると口語体になる.「まるで夏がきた

ような」は仮定法を用い，as if... の接続語句を用いる

〈解 答 例〉
(i) The thermometer showed 25 degrees here on the tenth of March. It was very hot, so we felt as if it were summer.

(ii) The thermometer went up to 25 degrees in this area on March 10th, and it was as hot as if summer were here with us.

☆

――〈例題 2〉――
ここ 2, 3 日，お天気がほんとうに変わりやすいですね．この空模様から判断すると，明日は雨かも知れませんよ．

■[語 句] 「変わりやすい」changeable, unsettled
■[考え方] 「ここ 2, 3 日」という期間の継続的状態は，現在完了形を用いる．「この空模様から判断すると」は既出の From the look of the sky とする．「雨かも知れない」は，It か We を主語に．「ね」や「よ」は訳出しない方が自然な表現である

〈解 答 例〉
(i) The weather has been very changeable for the last two or three days. From the look of the sky it may rain tomorrow.

(ii) The weather has been very unsettled for the past few days. From the way the sky looks, we may have rain tomorrow.

☆

――〈例題 3〉――
12 月 4 日の朝，雪がやんだ．雪は前日の朝から降りだして，夕方までに 15 センチほどつもっていた．

■[語句]「12月4日の朝」on the morning of December 4th /「夕方までに」by the evening /「15センチほどつもる」lie ～ centimeters deep *cf.*「雪が1メートルもつもった」The snow piled up about a meter. ともいう

■[考え方]「...前日の朝から降りだして」の時制は，「雪がやんだ」という過去から考え，過去完了形を用いる．最後の「つもっていた」も，同様に過去完了形にする

〈解　答　例〉

(i) On the morning of December 4th the snow stopped falling. It had begun to snow on the morning of the day before and had lain fifteen centimeters deep by the evening.

(ii) It stopped snowing on the morning of December 4th. Since the morning of the previous day, the snow had begun to fall and had reached a depth of fifteen centimeters by the evening.

┌──〈例題 4〉──
│ 近年，世界は異常気象状態にあるようだ．昨年アメリカでも，厳冬のはずだった長期予報がはずれて，まれにみる暖冬となった．
└──

■[語句]「近年」in recent years /「異常気象」unusual [extraordinary] weather /「長期予報」the long-range (weather) forecast

■[考え方] 第1文は「気象が世界中で異常である」と言い換え，The weather を主語にするのが最も簡単である．「厳冬のはずだった長期予報」は，「厳冬になるといった長期の天気予報」と解し，「天気予報」を主語にする．「はずれる」は，「正しくない」とか「当たらない」と考える．「まれにみる暖冬」は「異常な暖冬」か，「いままでのうちで最も暖い冬」などと訳す

第1章　天候・季節

〈解　答　例〉

(i) The weather seems to have been unusual all over the world in recent years.　In America, last year the long-term forecast said that they were going to have a severe winter, but it was not right.　In fact, it turned out to be an unusually mild winter there.

(ii) It seems that we have been having unusual weather worldwide for some years.　Last year in the United States, the long-range forecast that had predicted a severe winter, did not come true; in fact it proved to be one of the mildest winters they had ever had.

─〈例題 5〉─
越後は降雪地として有名であるが，冬の新潟市を訪れる人たちは，雪が意外と少ないのに驚くのではないかと思う．

■[語句]　「降雪地」an area where it snows a great deal
■[考え方]　「降雪地として有名」は「大雪で有名」とするか，「雪が降る地方としてよく知られている」と言い換える．「雪が意外と少ない」は，「雪が期待していたよりも少ない」と解する

〈解　答　例〉

(i) Echigo is famous for its heavy snowfalls, but some people who go to Niigata City in winter will probably be surprised that they have less snow than they expected.

(ii) Echigo is well known as a part of the country where it snows a lot, but I'm afraid that visitors to Niigata City in winter will be surprised to find that there is less snow there than they expected.

☆

―〈例題 6〉―
北日本は，冬季3ヵ月か4ヵ月，雪でおおわれる．くる日もくる日も，雪解けを待ちながら，家の中にこもらざるをえない．だから，北国の人々は，どんなささいな春のきざしにも躍り上がって喜ぶ．

■[語句]　「雪解け」the thawing of snow /「春のきざし」a sign of spring /「躍り上がって喜ぶ」jump for joy

■[考え方]　「待ちながら，家の中にこもる」の主語は，文頭の「北日本」から判断して，「そこに住む人々」とすればよい．第3文の「北国の人々」は代名詞を用いて表わす

〈解　答　例〉

(i) The northern part of Japan is covered with snow for three or four months in winter. People living there must stay at home each day, waiting for the thawing of the snow. So, any slight sign of spring makes them happy.

(ii) Northern Japan is under snow for three or four months of the year. The inhabitants there are forced to confine themselves to their houses day after day, waiting for the snow to thaw. That is why they jump for joy at any slight sign of spring.

第2章
衣・食・住

Check & Check

□衣食住 ⇨ food, clothing and shelter
　▶英語では,「食・衣・住」の順序が普通. clothes や houses は衣や住の全体を指さない

⟨ **Food** (食) ⟩
□1日に3度食事をする ⇨ have [eat] three meals a day
　▶*take* a meal はあまり使わない
□食事の仕度(した(く))をする ⇨ prepare a meal
　▶「食事を片づける」⇨ clear the table
□自炊する ⇨ cook for oneself, cook [fix] one's own meals
□間食をする ⇨ eat (a snack) between meals
□自由に～を取って食べる[飲む] ⇨ help oneself to ～

□食餌(しょく)療法を始める[している] ⇨ go [be] on a diet
　▶begin dieting ともいう. a meal は「1度の食物量」, a diet は「(栄養上からみた)食物の種類」の意

□自然食をとる ⇨ eat natural food

□菜食する ⇨ live on vegetables
　▶菜食主義の食事 ⇨ a vegetarian meal

□医者は私に食餌療法をさせた ⇨ The doctor put me on a diet.
　▶The doctor ordered me to go on a diet. ともいう

□お茶を飲みながら雑談する ⇨ chat [talk] over a cup of tea

□寿司を人におごる ⇨ treat one to [buy one] *sushi*
　▶one's treat として名詞用法で,「～のおごり」の意

□刺身を食べる ⇨ eat sliced raw fish
　▶米口語では sashimi として, そのまま用いている

□食べ物や着る物にうるさい ⇨ be particular about what one eats or wears
　▶「うるさい」を particular の代わりに hard to please とすると, 後は when it comes to one's food or clothes となる

□夕飯ができた ⇨ Supper is ready.

□食卓につく ⇨ sit down to table

□朝[昼, 夕]食をとる ⇨ have [eat] breakfast [lunch, dinner]
　▶breakfast, lunch, dinner などは, 普通は不可算名詞. しかし, 形容詞がついたり, 食事の種類をいうときは可算名詞扱いとなる.「急いで朝飯を食べる」have *a* hasty [hurried] breakfast / *a* Christmas dinner

□彼らは私を晩さんに招いた ⇨ They asked me to dinner.

□食事の作法 ⇨ table manners

第2章 衣・食・住

□目下，アフリカのある地方では食糧がひどく不足している ⇨ There is at present a serious food shortage in some parts of Africa.

□食が進む[進まない] ⇨ have a good [poor] appetite
　▶appetite は「食欲」ばかりか，「彼は知識欲が旺盛です」⇨ He has a great appetite for knowledge. のようにも用いる

□「卵はどのようにしましょうか」「半熟がいい」⇨ "How do you like your eggs?" "I like them soft-boiled."
　▶レストランなどでよく使う会話

□塩をこちらに回して下さい ⇨ Will you pass [hand] me the salt, please?
　▶食卓での会話．必ず salt には the をつける

□魚は消化によい ⇨ Fish is good for the digestion.

□彼は魚を生で食べるのに慣れている ⇨ He is used to eating fish raw.

□彼は酒に強い ⇨ He can drink a lot.
　▶「彼は酒に弱い」⇨ He can't drink much. / He gets drunk easily. 日本語をそのまま英語にし，"I'm weak in beer." といっても通じない．weak や strong は，"He is strong in French."（フランス語が達者です）などと「学科の能力」等について用いられる

□暴飲暴食する ⇨ eat and drink too much

□外食する ⇨ dine out, eat out

⟨ **Clothing**（衣）⟩

□着物を着る[脱ぐ] ⇨ put on [take off] one's clothes
　▶動作の表現．「試着する」は try on ～ という

□きれいな[ひどい]服装をしている ⇨ be finely [poorly]

dressed
　▶「彼女は白い服を着ている」⇨ She is dressed in white.＝ She is wearing a white dress.
　▶習慣的状態の表現

□妹は派手好きです ⇨ My sister likes dressing up in fancy clothes.

□その娘は赤い服が似合う ⇨ The girl looks good *in* a red dress.
　▶The red dress looks good *on* the girl. 両者とも同意であるが，前置詞の違いに注意. 次の他動詞 become を含む表現にも注意. The new dress becomes you.

□普段[晴れ]着 ⇨ everyday [Sunday] clothes
　▶「晴れ着」を Sunday best ともいう.「彼は晴れ着を着ている」⇨ He is in his Sunday best. 本来, 教会に行く服装のことをいうが, 現在では, よそ行きの着物のこと

□彼の服はすべて注文だ ⇨ He has all his suits made to order.
　▶「でき合いを買う」⇨ He buys all his suits ready-made.

□洋服のほうが和服よりも活動しやすい ⇨ Foreign clothes are easier to work in than Japanese clothes.
　▶work の代わりに, get around も用いられる. 前置詞 in が clothes にかかる
　▶「和服」を kimonos としてもよい

□この布は持ちがよい ⇨ This cloth wears well.

□あなたの洋服[靴]のサイズはいくつですか ⇨ What size of suit [shoes] do you wear?

□その靴はきつい ⇨ The shoes pinch me.

□目に日光を当てないようにサングラスをかけている ⇨ I wear

sunglasses to protect my eyes from the sunlight.
▶glass は「眼鏡」の意では，必ず複数形．a glass は「飲酒」の意．「ちょっと飲み過ぎた」⇨ I have had a glass too much.

〈 **Shelter**（住い）〉

□家を建てる ⇨ have [get] a house built
　▶「家を借りる」⇨ rent a house. 「貸し家」⇨《英》a house to let, 《米》a house for rent. 「新築」⇨ a newly-built house

□家事を切り盛りする ⇨ keep house
　▶この熟語では，house は無冠詞．cf. keep open house は「来客をいつでも歓迎する」意の熟語

□2階家 ⇨ a two-storeyed [-storied] house

□私の部屋は2階です ⇨《米》My room is on the second floor.
　▶英国では，1階を the ground floor, 2階を the first floor という

□彼の新築の家は洋風です ⇨ His new house is built in a foreign style.
　▶「日本風の家屋」⇨ a house in the Japanese style

□木造家屋は快適だが，火事になりやすい ⇨ Wooden houses are comfortable to live in, but catch fire easily.

□この分譲マンションはコンクリートの7階建てである ⇨ This condominium is a seven-storeyed concrete building.
　▶英国では，a flat という．「アパート」⇨ an apartment (house)

□この寮には便利な設備が何でもある ⇨ This dormitory has all the modern conveniences.

□団地 ⇨ housing development
　▶英国では，housing estate という

- □住宅不足を緩和する ⇨ ease the housing shortage
- □近くに2軒の新しいホテルが建設中です ⇨ There are two new hotels near here under construction.
- □高層建築地域 ⇨ a high-rise area
- □その建物がデパートに改造された ⇨ The building has been remodelled into a department store.
    - ▶「古い家を改築する」remodel an old house
- □下宿暮らしをする ⇨ live in lodgings
    - ▶この表現では，lodging は複数形.「友人の家に下宿している」⇨ I'm boarding at my friend's house. 賄(まかない)付き下宿のこと．なお，米国では，He is rooming with us. といえば賄付きでない下宿のこと
- □6畳の部屋 ⇨ a six-mat room
- □私は2階の寝室で寝ています ⇨ I sleep in the bedroom upstairs.
- □東京のベッドタウンに住んでいるので，あまり人が訪ねてこない ⇨ Since I live in the suburbs of Tokyo, I have few visitors.
    - ▶ベッドタウンは和製英語
- □我が家の良い所は南向きで，日当たりの良いことです ⇨ The good thing about my house is that it faces (to the) south and it is very sunny.
- □冷房している部屋 ⇨ an air-cooled room
    - ▶「冷暖房のあるバス」⇨ an air-conditioned bus
- □いつ新居に引っ越す計画ですか ⇨ What day are you planning to move *into* your new house?
    - ▶「大阪に引っ越す」⇨ move *to* Osaka

第2章 衣・食・住

□君の隣に住む ⇨ live next door to you
　▶「隣の人」a next-door neighbor.「1軒置いて隣」next door but one.「3軒置いて隣」three doors away

□電話を引く ⇨ have a telephone installed

□今度のアパートは水もお湯も出ます ⇨ My new apartment has both hot and cold water.

□ここにはまだガスがきていない ⇨ No gas is laid on here yet.

Let's Try

【I】 次の各英文が，それぞれ下の日本文に相当する意味になるように（　）内に適当な1語を補いなさい．

1. Please help (　　) to whatever you like.
　（どれでもお好きなものを取ってください）
2. He doesn't eat (　　) but natural food.
　（彼は自然食品以外は食べない）
3. The more you eat, the more weight you'll (　　).
　（食べれば食べるだけ太りますよ）
4. She couldn't make up her mind (　　) to wear to the party.
　（彼女はパーティーに何を着ていくか迷った）
5. The boy fell asleep with his clothes (　　).
　（その少年は服を着たまま寝てしまった）
6. He lives a few doors (　　).
　（彼は2, 3軒離れたところに住んでいる）
7. That child is wearing his shoes on the (　　) feet.
　（あの子は靴を逆にはいているよ）
8. I don't care (　　) heavy food.
　（胃にもたれる食事はだめです）

9. That girl doesn't look well (   ).
(あの娘は着ばえがしない)
10. I am wondering if you could put me (   ) for one night.
(君の家にひと晩泊めていただけますか)

■[考え方] 1. help=serve の意. 2. eat nothing but と同義に. 3. *put on* weight と同義. 4.「疑問詞+to 不定詞」の型. 5. with+O+前置詞の句. 6.「離れて」の副詞. 7.「間違っている」の形容詞. 8. care (   )=like 9. 過去分詞 10. put me (   )=provide food and lodging for me
■[解答] 1. yourself 2. anything 3. gain 4. what 5. on 6. away 7. wrong 8. for 9. dressed 10. up

【II】 次の語を並べ換えて，意味の通じる文をつくりなさい.
1. suggested, go, doctor, a, on, the, I, diet
2. exercise, appetite, give, a, an, little, you, will
3. something, can't, chocolate, I, without, is, do
4. my father, his breakfast, about, on, particular, time, very, exactly, is, having
5. shoes, them, without, never, trying, buy, first, on
6. people, look, they, down, because, dressed, don't, poorly, are, on

■[考え方] 1. suggested は，仮定法現在の節を従える. 2. A little exercise を主語に. 3. can't do without が慣用句. 4. particular about が頻出句. 5. try on shoes だが，代名詞 them の位置は？ 6. look down on が動詞句
■[解答] 1. The doctor suggested I go on a diet. 2. A little exercise will give you an appetite. 3. Chocolate is something I can't do without. 4. My father is very particular about having his breakfast exactly on time. 5. Never buy

shoes without trying them on first.　6. Don't look down on people because they are poorly dressed.

Let's Memorize

1. 洋食より和食のほうが好きです．
I prefer Japanese food to Western food.

2. 食欲がなくても，何か食べるようにしなさい．
Even if you don't have an appetite, you should try to eat something.

3. 夏は暑くてあまり食べる気がしない．
In summer it's so hot you don't feel like eating much.

4. 昨夜の牡蠣(か き)フライで，おなかをこわした．
The fried oysters last night upset me [my stomach].

5. 彼はよく食べるのに，少しも太らない．
Even though he eats a lot, he doesn't gain any weight at all.

6. あの娘はいつも質素だが，さっぱりしたなりをしている．
That girl is always plainly but neatly dressed.

7. この靴は僕にちょうどいい．
These shoes are just my size.

8. 今年は帽子がはやっている．
Hats are in fashion this year.

9. あの男子校は，生徒全員が制服を着ることにしている．
That boys' school requires every student to wear a uniform.

10. デパートで，でき合いの背広を買った．
I bought a ready-made suit at a department store.

11. 日本の個人の家はたいてい木造である.	Most private houses in Japan are built of wood.
12. 最近移った彼の新居は, 地下鉄の駅に近い.	The new house he recently moved into is near the subway station.
13. この部屋はストーブがついているから暖かい.	This room is warm because the heater is on.
14. この辺は家が建て込んでいる.	This neighborhood is crowded with houses.
15. この新しい高層ビルは, どんな地震でも大丈夫であるといわれている.	This new skyscraper is said to be able to withstand any earthquake.

Exercises

────〈例題 1〉────
「服装や身だしなみにだらしない人間は他の事にもだらしがないものだ」というのが私の祖父の口ぐせでした.

■[語句]「身だしなみ」personal appearance /「だらしのない」careless, sloppy, untidy

■[考え方]「だらしのない人間」は, 関係代名詞を用い, a person who is ~ とするか, 接続詞を用い, If a person is ~ とすることができる.「口ぐせ」は, 単に「常にいった」とすれば十分である

〈解 答 例〉

(i) My grandfather always said, "A person who is careless about his clothes and personal appearance is also careless about other things."

(ii) My grandfather used to say that if a person was careless and untidy about his clothes and personal appearance, he was careless about other things, too.

──〈例題 2〉──
　若い女の人たちが，ときどき食堂で野菜サラダだけをとっているのを見かける．レタスとキュウリに食塩をふりかけ，モクモクと食べる彼女たちは，ご飯を食べると太ると思うから食べないのである．

■[語 句]　「野菜サラダ」vegetable salads /「レタス」lettuce /「キュウリ」cucumber /「～に食塩をふりかける」sprinkle salt over ～

■[考え方]　「女の人たちが～とっているのを見かける」は，女性を主語にし受身形で，Young women are seen eating ～ とするか，不定詞構文を使い，It is common to see young women eating ～ と表現する．第2文は，「食塩をふりかけ，～と食べる」で区切って，「ご飯を食べると太る～」を独立させ，できる限り日本文を短く切って，英語に直すのも和文英訳のひとつのコツである

〈解　答　例〉

(i) In restaurants, young women are often seen eating only vegetable salads. These women, after sprinkling some salt over lettuce or cucumber, eat their salads quietly [intently]. They will not touch any rice, which they think will make them fat.

(ii) It is common to see young women eating only vegetable salads in restaurants. They eat lettuce or cucumber sprinkled with salt, but avoid rice (at all cost), simply because they think rice will make them gain weight.

☆

―――〈例題 3〉―――
　わたしは，どこの国に滞在するときにも，できるだけその土地の食べ物で暮らすように心がけている．そのほうが，日本食に高い金を払うより，経済的であるのはもちろん，概してうまいものが食べられるからである．

■[語 句]　「土地の食べ物」local food /「〜に心がける」make a point of 〜ing, try to 〜 /「経済的」economical /「概して」generally

■[考え方]　「そのほうが...より経済的である」は「その土地の食べ物を食べることが，日本食に高い金を払うより経済的である」とするか，「〜より費用がかからない」とする．「そのほうが A はもちろん，概して B だからである」は This is *not only because* A, *but also because* B の相関接続詞で結ぶと，全体がバランスのとれた英文となる

〈解　答　例〉

（i）　When I stay in any foreign country, I always try to eat as much local food as I can. This is not only because it is more economical to eat local food than to pay a lot of money for Japanese food, but also because generally local food tastes delicious.

（ii）　No matter what foreign country I stay in, I always make a point of eating as much local food as possible. Of course, it costs you less to eat local food than to pay a large sum of money for Japanese food, and generally it is also possible to find good things to eat.

第2章 衣・食・住

―〈例題 4〉―――
飲食店でいつも閑古(かん)鳥が鳴いているところと，客が次から次へと立て込んでいるところがある．いずれも同じようなものを食べさせる店なのに．それにはいろいろ理由があるだろうが，結局は味が勝負である．

■[語 句]「客が次から次へと」a constant stream of customers /「立て込んでいる」be crowded (with) /「食べさせる」serve /「結局」after all

■[考え方]「閑古鳥が鳴いている」は，「客が少ない」とし，「立て込んでいる」は「大勢の客がいる」とすれば，十分意味の通る英文になる．「...ところと，～ところがある」は相関する語句を用い，*some* restaurants..., while *others* ～ とする．「味が勝負である」は，「料理がおいしいかどうかが，この商売では唯一の決定的要因である」と英訳するか，「味がいいかどうかが，最も大切である」と言い換える．要は，日本文をそのまま英訳せず，その意味をできる限りやさしい語句で表現することである

〈解 答 例〉

(i) There are few customers in some restaurants, while there are a lot of customers in others. They serve almost the same kind of dishes, though. There are many reasons for this, but the most important thing is whether the food tastes good or not.

(ii) Some restaurants are almost always deserted or empty, while others are crowded with a constant stream of customers, although, in either case, the kind of food served is much the same. There may be various reasons for this, but whether the food tastes nice is the only deciding [determining] factor in this business.

┌──〈例題 5〉──────────────┐
│　わたくしは上京するたびに街の変わりようの早さに驚い │
│てしまう．30 階を越すビルディング工事があちこちで行な │
│われている．　　　　　　　　　　　　　　　　　　　　 │
└─────────────────────┘

■[考え方]　「街の変わりようの早さに驚く」は，「街が早く変わっていることを知って驚く」と節にするか，「街の中の速い変化に驚く」として句にするか，2 通りに書くことができる．「街」は，Tokyo の繰り返しを避けるため，「その都市」とする．「30 階を越すビルディング工事が...行なわれている」は，「30 階以上のビルがあちこちで工事中である」と解す

〈 解　答　例 〉

　(i) Every time I come to Tokyo, I am surprised that the city has changed so quickly. Buildings over 30 stories high are being constructed here and there.

　(ii) Whenever I come up to Tokyo, the rapid change in the city surprises me. Buildings of over 30 storeys are under construction in various places.

第3章
健康・病気

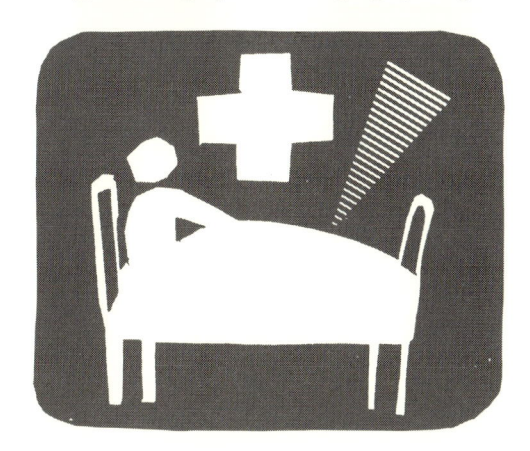

Check & Check

□[不]健康である ⇨ be in good [poor, bad] health
　▶in good condition は「運動選手や事物の状態」に用いるのが普通. cf.「その品物が破損せずに着いた」⇨ The goods arrived in good condition.

□体調を保つ ⇨ keep [stay] in shape
　▶「好調を維持する」意.「体調を整える」は, get in shape という. これらの表現では, shape は無冠詞.「体調をくずしている」⇨ be out of shape

□健康に注意する ⇨ take good care of oneself, be careful about one's health
　▶人と別れるときなどに聞かれる,「達者でね」は, Keep well. という

□元気がないですね．どうかなさいましたか．⇨ You aren't looking well. What is the matter with you?
　▶look *well* は健康上，look *good* [nice] は容姿，外観についていう

□健康を増進する ⇨ improve one's health

□健康を害する ⇨ injure [ruin, lose] one's health

□風邪が今はやっている ⇨ There are a lot of colds going around now.

□彼はひどい風邪で学校を休んだ ⇨ He stayed home from school because of a bad cold.
　▶風邪などで「学校を休む」という動作的表現は，現実に家庭にいるわけだから，stay *home* from school というのが普通．ただし，「彼は風邪で１週間ほど学校を休んでいます」という状態的表現は，He has been absent from school about a week because of a cold. となる

□雨にぬれると，風邪をひきますよ ⇨ If you get wet in the rain, you will catch (a) cold.
　▶catch (a) cold は，未来・過去時制に用いられる．「彼は風邪をひいています」は，He *has* a cold. という

□病気が治る ⇨ recover from [get over] an illness
　▶「風邪が治る」⇨ get over [get rid of] one's cold.「病気が快方に向かう」は，病人が主語のときには，get better, 病状が主語のときには take a turn for the better という

□父の病状は快方に向かった ⇨ My father's condition has taken a change for the better.

□風邪は万病のもと ⇨ A cold may develop into all kinds of illness(es).

□健康診断を受ける ⇨ have a medical checkup

▶この句の medical は省略されることがある.「健康診断を受けに病院に行く」⇨ go to the hospital for a checkup
□ ひどく[ちょっと]頭が痛い ⇨ have a bad [slight] headache
　▶歯痛, 腹痛 (a toothache, a stomachache) にも, 同じ表現が使われる
□ のどが痛い ⇨ have a sore throat
　▶sore は形容詞.「痛む」(painful) の意
□ 昨晩は激しい歯痛でよく眠れなかった ⇨ Last night I couldn't sleep properly because of a very severe toothache.
□ 転地する ⇨ go (to a place) for a change of air
　▶for a change は, 口語で「気分を変えて」の意
□ 彼はどこか具合が悪い ⇨ There is something wrong with him.
　▶「調子が悪い」の意の out of order は, 機械や公共の施設が「故障」の意に用いられる
□ 彼は肺結核にかかっているらしい ⇨ He seems to be suffering from tuberculosis [TB].
　▶「肺結核」を俗に consumption ともいう. 病名は, 無冠詞
□ 彼は重態で, 医者は全快の見込みがないといっている ⇨ He is seriously ill, and the doctor says that there is no hope of recovery.
□ 彼は耳が遠い ⇨ He is hard of hearing.
　▶「聴力を失う」⇨ lose one's hearing＝become deaf.「彼女は猩紅(しょうこう)熱のため聴力を失った」⇨ She lost her hearing through scarlet fever.
□ 熱が出る ⇨ have [run] a temperature, have a fever, become feverish

▶take *one's* temperature は「熱を計る」意
□彼はたった100メートル走っても息が切れた ⇨ He was out of breath after running only 100 meters.
　▶「息を殺す」⇨ hold one's breath /「息を深くつく」⇨ draw [take] a deep breath
□人に応急手当てをする ⇨ give first aid to a person
□彼女は先週肺ガンの手術を受けた ⇨ Last week she had [underwent] an operation for lung cancer.
　▶「胃ガン」⇨ stomach [gastric] cancer
　▶「その外科医は父の盲腸炎の手術をした」⇨ The surgeon performed an operation on my father for appendicitis. 動詞表現: The surgeon operated on my father for appendicitis.
　▶「手術する」は，患者が主語のときは *have* an operation, 医師が主語になると，*perform* an operation と動詞が異なることに注意
□太る[やせる] ⇨ gain [lose] weight
　▶形容詞の fat や thin は病的な意味をもつことがある．なお，「トムは病気で体重が減った」を英訳して，Tom lost *his* weight because of his illness. とするのは誤り. his weight の his をとる
□長生きする ⇨ live long, enjoy longevity
　▶「日本人の平均寿命が延びるだろう」⇨ The average life expectancy of the Japanese will increase.
□長寿の秘訣 ⇨ the secret of longevity
□入院する ⇨ go to [enter] the hospital. 《米》be hospitalized
　▶退院する ⇨ come out of [leave] the hospital. 《英》では，定冠詞 the を省く
□ジムは病院で治療を受けている ⇨ Jim is undergoing medi-

cal treatment in the hospital.
▶「治療を受ける」は undergo a cure も用いられる．冠詞の有無に注意

□私は昨日，小林君を見舞いに病院に行った ⇨ I went to the hospital yesterday to see Mr. Kobayashi.
▶ask [inquire] after a person は，看護婦や医者から病人の容体を間接的に聞くこと

□この食物は胃にもたれる ⇨ This food lies heavy on my stomach.

□昨日は胃の具合が悪くて一日寝ていた ⇨ I stayed in bed all day yesterday because I had a stomach upset.
▶この upset は「体(特に胃)の異常」の意の名詞
▶「下痢する」を have diarrh(o)ea [dàiərí:ə] というが，日常生活では，「胃腸の具合が悪い」と表現する方が上品

□医者にみてもらう ⇨ see [consult] a doctor
▶「医者を呼ぶ」⇨ call in [send for] the doctor
▶「内科医」⇨ a physician.「外科医」⇨ a surgeon.「一般開業医」a general practitioner.「心臓専門医」a heart specialist

□父は医師の忠告で禁煙した ⇨ My father has given up [quit] smoking on his doctor's advice [at his doctor's suggestion].
▶「これは医師の命令です」のときは，This is (the) doctor's orders. という

□風邪の薬を飲んでいるの？ ⇨ Are you taking the medicine for your cold?
▶「水薬」以外，*drink* the medicine は誤り．「熱[胃]の薬」⇨ a medicine for fever [indigestion]

□その薬は何に効くの？ ⇨ What is the medicine good for?

□この薬を飲めば風邪が治るだろう ⇨ This medicine will cure you of your cold.
　▶「薬が効いた」⇨ The medicine worked.

□働き[食べ]すぎないように注意する ⇨ be careful not to work [eat] too much

□健康のためにジョギングをする ⇨ jog for one's health

□歩くことこそ君の病気にはいちばんよい療法だ ⇨ Walking is the best remedy for your disease.

□「今朝はご気分はいかがですか」「昨日よりずっとよくなりました」⇨ "How are you feeling this morning?" "I am feeling much better than yesterday."
　▶I couldn't feel better. は「気分最高」の意で，しばしば使われる

□昨夜は1時間しか眠っていないので，今日はとても眠い ⇨ Since I had only an hour's sleep last night, I am very sleepy today.
　▶この表現では，sleep の前に some, much などの形容詞が必要．have [get] a good sleep とすれば，「ぐっすり眠る」の意

□睡眠不足 ⇨ lack of sleep

□授業中，居眠りする ⇨ doze off in class
　▶doze off は，「うっかり眠る」の意．cf.「昼寝する」⇨ have [take] a nap

□病人 ⇨ a sick person
　▶a patient（患者）は医師に対して用いられる語

□仮病(けびょう)を使う ⇨ pretend to be ill [sick]
　▶「彼は本当は病気ではなく，仮病を使っていた」⇨ He was not really ill; he was only pretending.

第3章 健康・病気

☐山田先生は京都で医者を開業している ⇒ Dr. Yamada practices medicine in Kyoto.
  ▶この場合，medicine は無冠詞．cf.「弁護士を開業している」⇒ practice law．「新潟で藤原先生は，はやっている」⇒ Dr. Fujiwara has a large practice in Niigata.
  ▶この practice は，不定冠詞と形容詞をつける

☐病気が軽い[重い] ⇒ be slightly [seriously] ill.
  ▶「危篤だ」⇒ be critically [dangerously] ill.「病気になる」は fall ill, be taken ill というが，普通，get ill がよく用いられる

☐海岸へ旅行すれば身体に良いだろう ⇒ Your trip to the seaside will do you good.
  ▶この good の前に much や a lot of などがつくことがある

☐早くご全快することを祈ります ⇒ I hope you will make a quick recovery.
  ▶「祈る」は，宗教的な意味の pray よりも，hope がよい

☐伝染病 ⇒ a contagious [an infectious] disease
  ▶「慢性病」⇒ a chronic disease.「急性病」an acute disease

☐脳卒中の発作を起こす ⇒ have a stroke
  ▶「脳こうそく」⇒ (a) cerebral infarction

☐心不全で死亡する ⇒ die of heart failure
  ▶die *of* は主として病気，die *from* は衰弱，不注意，負傷などの原因を表わす．「永眠する」という婉曲な表現として pass away も用いられる

☐内藤さんの健康を祝して乾杯しよう ⇒ Let's drink to Mr. Naito's health.
  ▶なお，「内藤さんのために乾杯」は，Let's drink a toast to Mr. Naito. というのが最も一般的．

Let's Try

【Ⅰ】次の各文が，それぞれ下の日本文に相当する意味になるように（　　）の中に適当な1語を補いなさい.

1. She seems to be putting on a little (　　) lately.
   (彼女は最近太り気味だ)
2. I've stopped drinking (　　) my doctor's advice.
   (医者のすすめで禁酒している)
3. The child often gets an upset (　　).
   (その子はよくおなかをこわす)
4. A contagious disease (　　) out in that town after the flood.
   (あの町では洪水のあと伝染病が発生した)
5. She is (　　) from healthy.
   (彼女は健康どころではない)
6. I've been (　　) up since Christmas with a bad cough.
   (クリスマスから咳(せき)がひどく，床についている)
7. I finally got (　　) of my cold.
   (風邪がやっと治った)
8. Most people (　　) two or three colds a year.
   (たいてい人は年に2，3度風邪をひく)
9. Try to get yourself in good (　　) before the game.
   (試合までに体調を整えておきなさい)
10. The medicine apparently (　　); my headache is much better.
    (薬が効いたとみえ，頭痛がおさまってきた)

■[考え方]　1.「体重」.名詞.　2.「したがって」.前置詞.　3.

「胃」. **4.** 火災・戦争・疫病が突然発生する意の動詞句. **5.** (　　) from で否定の意. **6.** 他動詞 lay の過去分詞. **7.** got (　　) of = got over. **8.** have か catch か. **9.** health と同義語. **10.** = be effective.
■[解答] 1. weight 2. on 3. stomach 4. broke 5. far 6. laid 7. rid 8. catch 9. shape 10. works

【II】 次の (a), (b) の英文の意味がだいたい同じになるように, 空所に適当な1語を補いなさい.
1. (a) Hard work will affect his health.
　(b) Hard work will (　　) on his health.
2. (a) Illness prevented her from attending school yesterday.
　(b) Illness kept her (　　) from school yesterday.
3. (a) If you don't take vitamins, you will have a disease.
　(b) Lack of vitamins will (　　) you to fall ill.
4. (a) You'll catch cold if you don't watch out.
　(b) Take (　　) not to catch cold.
5. (a) The baby is the picture of health.
　(b) The baby is in (　　) health.

■[考え方] **1.**「悪い影響を与える」. 動詞句. **2.** prevent も keep も V+O+from+〜ing 形の文型があるが, この keep は, from のあとに 〜ing がこない. **3.**「引き起こす」 **4.** Be careful. と同義. **5.**「完全な」
■[解答] 1. tell 2. away 3. cause 4. care 5. perfect [excellent]

【III】 次の各文が応答文になるような疑問文を作りなさい.
1. The fish upset my stomach last night.

2. She has been ill for a week.
3. No, nothing is the matter.
4. I feel much better than yesterday.
5. Because I was sick in bed yesterday.

■[考え方] 1.「何を食べておなかをこわしたのか」 2.「1週間」の期間がポイント. 3. the matter は wrong と同義.「何か困ったこと」 4. ここでは気分を聞いている. 5. Because に対して, Why で聞く.

■[解答] 1. What kind of food upset your stomach last night? 2. How long has she been ill? 3. What's the matter with you? 4. How do you feel today? 5. Why did you stay away from school yesterday? / Why were you absent yesterday?

Let's Memorize

1. 健康が何より大切だ.	Health is more important than anything else.
2. おかげさまで, 私は元気に暮らしています.	I'm getting along quite well, thanks.
3. 毎日規則正しく運動しているので, 健康でいられるのだと思う.	I think getting regular exercise every day keeps me in good health.
4. 歯医者に行って, 虫歯を抜いてもらった.	I went to the dentist and had a decayed tooth pulled.
5. 風邪をひいて, 熱がでた.	I caught a cold and developed a fever.
6. 静かにしていないと, 熱が上がるよ.	Your temperature will go up if you don't stay in bed.

第3章 健康・病気

7. 風邪には，この薬がよく効く．
   This medicine is really effective against colds.

8. 彼女はやっと全快して，床(とこ)を離れた．
   At last she completely recovered and was able to get out of bed.

9. 病気になってはじめて，病人の気持がわかるものだ．
   You don't realize how it feels [what it is] to be ill until you get sick.

10. 背中がひどく痛みます．
    I have a terrible pain in my back.

11. 彼女の病気は峠(とうげ)を越した．
    She got through the critical period of her illness.

12. 彼女はもう10年間も病気とたたかっている．
    She has been struggling with illness for the past ten years.

13. 筋力強化のため毎日つとめて体操している．
    I try to do exercise every day to strengthen my muscles.

14. 医者が彼を診察したが，どこも悪くなかった．
    The doctor gave him a checkup, and found nothing wrong.

Exercises

〈例題 1〉
健康を維持するには，適度に運動し，十分な睡眠をとることが大切である．

■[語句]「健康を維持する」maintain health, keep in good health /「適度に運動する」get moderate exercise, exercise moderately /「十分な睡眠をとる」have a good sleep, sleep well
■[考え方]「...するには」は,「するためには」という目的を表わす in order to do を使えばよい.「とることが大切」は,「It is＋形容詞＋to 不定詞」の文型を用いる.「運動をすること」と「睡眠をとること」の2つは,不定詞で表わす.また,全文を,「適当な運動と十分な睡眠は健康に欠くことができない」と解し,英訳するのも手

〈解 答 例〉

(i) In order to keep in good health, it is important to exercise moderately and sleep well.

(ii) Moderate exercise and sufficient sleep are indispensable for good health.

☆

―〈例題 2〉――
「もしきみがタバコをやめたら,もっと健康になれるのに」と,医者はいつも忠告してくれるのですが,どうもやめられなくて困っています.

■[語句]「タバコをやめる」give up smoking /「困っている」be annoyed
■[考え方]「やめたら,～なのに」は,仮定法過去か,現在時制の2通りに訳すことができる.「忠告する」は単に「いう」とする.「～して困っている」は,「～なので困っている」と考えるか,「困ったことには～です」と解し,The trouble is that ...が慣用表現

〈解 答 例〉

(i) The doctor always said, " If you give up smoking,

it will make you much healthier." I am annoyed because I can't quit (smoking).

(ii) The doctor said, "If you gave up smoking, you would be in better health." The trouble is, however, that I find it hard to quit.

☆

─〈例題 3〉─
　健康は富にまさると人はよく言うが，実際に病気になってみなければ，この諺(ことわざ)の正しいことに気づかない．

■[語句]「健康は富にまさる」Health is above [more important than] wealth. /「この諺の正しいこと」the truth of this proverb

■[考え方]「～しなければ，...ない」は，「～するまでは，...できない」か，「病気になって初めて，...が理解できる」と肯定的な表現に直すことができる

〈解　答　例〉

(i) People often say that health is better than wealth, but none of them (can) understand how true this proverb is until they get ill.

(ii) People often say that health is more important than wealth, but few of them can realize the truth of this proverb until they actually become ill.

☆

─〈例題 4〉─
　彼によると，長生きの秘訣は細かいことにくよくよせず，規則正しい生活を送ることにあるという．

■[語句]「長生きの秘訣」the secret of longevity, the key

to long life /「細かいこと」small things, trifles /「くよくよする」worry about /「規則正しい生活を送る」lead [live] a routine life

■[考え方]「彼によると」は「彼がいう」とする.「～せず, ...にある」は対照関係になく not ～, but... は使えない

〈解　答　例〉

(i)　He says that the key to long life is not to worry about small things, and to live a routine life.

(ii)　He says that the secret of longevity is to lead a well-regulated life and not to worry about trifles.

☆

───〈例題 5〉───
　彼が病気になったとき, だれも彼の面倒を見てくれませんでした. 老人になって話し相手がひとりもいなかったら, さびしいだろう.

■[語　句]「面倒を見る」take care of, look after /「話し相手」a person to talk to

■[考え方]「だれも...ない」は, everyone とすると部分否定となり, 誤り. これは全面否定なので, No one を主語にする.「老人になって話し相手がひとりもいない」は,「老人が話し相手をもたない」とするか,「話し相手のいない老人は」と訳す

〈解　答　例〉

(i)　When he got sick, there wasn't anyone to take care of him. If an old person has nobody to talk to, he will feel very lonely.

(ii)　No one took care of him when he fell ill. An elderly person who has nobody to talk to would be very lonely.

第4章
人生・生活・時間

Check & Check

〈人生・生活〉

□人生観 ⇨ one's view of life, the way one views [looks at] life

□家庭生活 ⇨ family [home] life, domestic life

□生活水準を向上させる ⇨ improve [raise] one's standard of living

□文筆で生計をたてる ⇨ make [earn] a [one's] living by writing
　▶make [earn] a [one's] livelihood も同義の句

□日本は物価が高いので，収入内でやりくりするのが楽じゃない ⇨ Since commodity prices are high in Japan, it is

not easy to make (both) ends meet.
- □生活が楽である[に困っている] ⇨ be in easy [needy] circumstances
    - ▶be well [comfortably] off, be badly off も同義.
    - ▶この circumstances は,「(人の財産・収入に関する)身上, 境遇, 暮らし向き」の意
- □彼は貧しい家庭に生まれた ⇨ He was born of poor parents.
    - ▶「生まれる」意の'born'が borne となるのは, 次の (a), (b) の場合である
    - (a) His wife has *borne* him three children.
        (彼の妻は彼との間に3人の子を生んだ)
    - (b) He was *borne* by an English woman.
        (彼はイギリスの女性から生まれた)
    - すなわち, (a) 助動詞 have のあと, (b) 受動態で by+母親の形の前に置かれるとき
    - ▶彼は金持に生まれた ⇨ He was born rich.
- □その女性は生まれがよい ⇨ The woman is of high birth.
    - ▶She is a woman of high birth. ともいう
- □彼は年のわりに若くみえる ⇨ He looks young considering his age.
    - ▶considering=for で, 前置詞.「~年より若くみえる」は, He looks younger than he really is. ともいえる
- □彼は学生たちの間で評判がいい ⇨ He has a good reputation with his students.
    - ▶He is popular with [among] his students. も同義. popular *with* は, 彼と学生とを対立的にとらえ, 学生に日ごろから人気のあることを端的に述べているのに対し, popular *among* では, 比較的大勢の学生の間に彼の人気が広まっているという感じを表わす
- □人生[物事]の明るい[暗い]面を見る ⇨ look on the bright

第4章 人生・生活・時間

[dark] side of life [things]

☐ 物事をまじめに[のんびり]受けとる ⇨ take things seriously [easy]
　▶ take it easy は「ムリするな」の意に用いられる

☐ 祖父は気むずかしい ⇨ My grandfather is hard to please.
　▶「付き合いにくい」⇨ He is hard to get along with.

☐ ジェリーは画家として大いに将来有望だ ⇨ Jerry has [shows] great promise as a painter.
　▶ この promise は無冠詞. Jerry has a bright future before him as a painter. も同意表現

☐ 一生の友を得る ⇨ make lifelong friends

☐ 収入以上の生活をする ⇨ live beyond one's means [income]
　▶ この means は複数扱い.「収入内で生活する」⇨ live within one's means [income]

☐ 彼は貧しいとき, 借金していた ⇨ He was in debt when he was poor.
　▶ debt は無冠詞, 単数扱い.「借金がない」を out of debt という

☐ 生きがいを感じる ⇨ find one's life worth living

☐ 充実した生活を送る ⇨ have [live, lead] a full life
　▶ この表現では, 通例不定冠詞 a と形容詞をつけて用いる

☐ 辛酸(しんさん)をなめる ⇨ go through many hardships

☐ 栄枯盛衰 ⇨ ups and downs of life

☐ 年相応に振舞う ⇨ act one's age
　▶「年相応に見える」⇨ look one's age

☐ 十代のはじめ[後半]の娘 ⇨ a girl in her early [late] teens

□成年に達する ⇨ come of age, reach manhood

□私の娘は若いアメリカの医者と婚約している ⇨ My daughter is engaged to a young American doctor.

□彼はイギリス人の娘と昨年結婚した ⇨ He married an English girl last year.
　▶この marry は他動詞. He married very young. の marry は自動詞

□彼はそんなことには経験がない ⇨ He has no experience in such an affair.

□人間は経験から学ぶ ⇨ People learn from [by] experience.

□彼らの銀婚式をあげる ⇨ celebrate their silver wedding

□男[女]の赤ん坊 ⇨ a baby boy [girl]
　▶幼児 ⇨ an infant. 子供 ⇨ a child. 青年 ⇨ an adolescent. 成人 ⇨ an adult, a grown-up. 老人 ⇨ an elderly person
　▶60歳以上を, 特に a senior citizen ということがある

□高齢である ⇨ be advanced in age
　▶高齢で死ぬ ⇨ die at an advanced age, die very old cf. die young

□母は75歳で死んだ ⇨ My mother died aged [at the age of] seventy-five.
　▶この aged は [éidʒd] と発音する. cf. [éidʒid]

□葬式が昨日行なわれた ⇨ The funeral service was held [conducted] yesterday.

□焼死[凍死, 餓死]する ⇨ be burnt [frozen, starved] to death

□喪(も)に服する ⇨ go into mourning
　▶喪があける ⇨ come out of mourning

第4章　人生・生活・時間

□かなりの高給をとる ⇨ get [make] a good salary
　▶salary は,「専門的な職業にたずさわる者に定期的に与えられる給料」. wages は「手職の労務者などの賃金」をいう

□彼は大勢の家族を養う ⇨ He has a large family to support.

□妻は家計に赤字を出さないように苦労している ⇨ My wife is trying hard to balance our household budget.
　▶「予算をたてる」⇨ make a budget. budget は,「(国家, 家庭などの)予算(額)」の意. cf.「赤字を出さないようにする」⇨ balance the budget＝make ends meet

□先月昇給した ⇨ I got [had] a pay raise last month.
　▶《英》では raise の代わりに rise を用いる. 動詞表現：I had my pay raised last month.

□父は60歳で停年退職し, 今は年金で暮らしている. ⇨ My father retired at the age of 60, and now lives on a pension.

〈時　間〉

□何時ですか ⇨ Do you have the time?
　▶必ず定冠詞 the をつける. 時刻を尋ねる表現には他に, Have you got the time? とか What time do you have? などがある

□私の時計は正確です ⇨ My watch keeps good time.
　▶My watch keeps time very well. ともいう. この表現では, time は無冠詞

□この時計は3分進んで[遅れて]いる ⇨ This watch is three minutes fast [slow].

□この時計は1日に5秒ずつ進む[遅れる] ⇨ This watch gains [loses] five seconds a day.

□時計は 5 時 5 分を指していた ⇨ The clock said [showed] five minutes past five.
□僕の時計は狂っている ⇨ My watch has gone wrong.
□時計が 11 時を打った ⇨ The clock has struck eleven.
□テレビの時報で時計を合わせる ⇨ set the watch by the TV time signal
□間に合うように来てください ⇨ I wish you would come in time.
□列車がきっちり時間通り運行している ⇨ The trains run exactly on time.
□夕食後, 英語の勉強をして, 2 時間過ごした ⇨ After dinner I spent two hours studying English.
　▶spend＋時間, 金額など＋～ing の文型に注意
□日曜日には退屈しのぎに何をなさいますか ⇨ How do you manage to kill time on Sundays?
　▶kill time は「時間をつぶす」の意
□ゆっくり食事しなさい ⇨ Take your time when eating your meals.
□彼の家を見つけるのにずいぶん時間がかかった ⇨ It took me a long time to find his house.
　▶この time は不可算名詞だが, 形容詞がつくと不定冠詞 a を伴う
□長くたたないうちに, 彼が顔を見せた ⇨ It was not long before he showed up.
　▶It was long before he showed up. は He was (a) long (time) (in) showing up. と同義で, 「彼はなかなか顔を見せなかった」の意

第4章 人生・生活・時間

□今日の午後，テニスする時間あるかい ⇨ Do you have time to play tennis this afternoon?
　▶この表現では，time は無冠詞

□昨夜のパーティーは楽しかった ⇨ I had a good time at the party last night.
　▶time に不定冠詞 a と形容詞をつける

□彼はロンドンの生活に適応するのに苦労した ⇨ He had a hard time adjusting himself to living in London.
　▶have a hard time 〜ing は「〜するのに苦労する」の意の熟語．cf. have difficulty [trouble] 〜ing も同意表現

□彼は機を失せず，その仕事を申し込んだ ⇨ He lost no time (in) applying for the job.
　▶lose [waste] no time (in) 〜ing は「すぐに〜する」の意

□もうそろそろ学校へ行く時間だ ⇨ It's about time (that) you left for school.
　▶It's about time のあとの節は，仮定法過去時制を従える

□彼は約束の時間に遅れた ⇨ He was behind time for his appointment.
　▶「約束の時間よりも早く」は ahead of time という

□彼は今朝，6時30分の急行に1分のところで乗り遅れた ⇨ He missed the 6:30 express by a minute this morning.
　▶6:30 は six-thirty と読む
　▶この by は「時間の差」を表わす

□君の都合のよい時に家に遊びに来ませんか ⇨ Why don't you come over to our place whenever it is convenient for you?
　▶convenient は，人間は主語にならない

□駅へ行くのにどのくらいかかりますか ⇨ How long will it take to get to the station?
　▶it takes...to 不定詞は,「時間・労力などを必要とする」意の頻出構文

□そこまで徒歩で20分, バスだと5分です ⇨ It will take twenty minutes to walk there, but five minutes by bus.

□東京に移り住んでから15年近くです ⇨ It has been [is] almost fifteen years since I came to live in Tokyo.
　▶「～してから,（何年）になる」は, It has been [is]...since ～ の構文を用いる．この場合, since の前の節は, 現在完了形[現在形], since の後の節は過去形を用いる

□ボストンを訪れたのは今度が初めてです ⇨ This is the first time (that) I have ever visited Boston.
　▶現在までの「経験」を表わす．This is the first time は現在時制, あとに [have ever＋過去分詞], または, [ever＋過去時制] の両方が用いられる．単文では, This is my first visit to Boston. となる

□駅でタクシーに乗って初めて列車に傘を置き忘れたことに気がついた ⇨ It was not till I took a taxi at the station that I noticed I had left my umbrella on the train.
　▶「...するまでは～しない」の It is not till [until]...that ～ はやや形式ばった文で, 会話ではあまり用いられない．上の文を口語では, I left my umbrella on the train. I wasn't aware of it at the time. I realized it for the first time when I took a taxi at the station. となる

□6時の急行が出るまで十分時間がある ⇨ We have plenty of time before the six o'clock express leaves.
　▶「6時10分の急行」は the 6:10 express という

□彼は時間にとても正確だ ⇨ He is very punctual.

第4章 人生・生活・時間

☐彼らは時間の観念がない ⇨ They have no idea of time.

☐そこへ行くには, 2時間ぐらい見ておきなさい ⇨ You should give yourself about two hours to get there.
　▶この give [allow] yourself は「時間の余裕を与える」の意

☐10分ほどお時間をさいていただけませんか ⇨ Would you mind sparing me ten minutes of your time?

☐時間のたつのも忘れて語り合った ⇨ We talked and forgot all about the passage of time.

☐今日は, 3時間目に数学がある ⇨ We have mathematics in the third period today.

☐英語の授業は週に4時間ある ⇨ English class meets four hours a week.

☐来[先]週の今日 ⇨ a week from [ago] today
　▶this day week または today week は,「来週[先週]の今日」のどちらの意味にとるかは文脈による

☐一日中 ⇨ all day [long], all through the day
　▶先日 ⇨ the other day / 一日おきに ⇨ every other day / 来る日も来る日も ⇨ day after day /「日増しに」⇨ day by day / 1日か2日で ⇨ in a day or two / 近いうちに ⇨ shortly, one of these days / 近い将来に ⇨ in the near future / 近頃 ⇨ these days, nowadays, lately, recently (lately, recently は, 現在完了形及び過去形の動詞と共に用いられるのが普通)

☐時間の許す限り, お手伝いします ⇨ I will help you as long as time permits.

☐私は時間に追われる生活がつくづくいやになった ⇨ I got fed up with a life in which I was always pressed for time.

□久しぶりですね ⇨ I haven't seen you for a long time [for an age].
　▶It's been a long time since I saw you last. も同義
□彼から久しぶりに手紙をもらった ⇨ I had a letter from him for the first time in quite some time [in a long time].
□遅くなりますから，もうおいとまいたします ⇨ Since it is getting late, I'm afraid I must be going [leaving].
□残り時間が少なくなってきた ⇨ Time is running out.
　▶時間切れです ⇨ Time is up.

Let's Try

【Ⅰ】 次の各英文が，それぞれ下の日本文に相当する意味になるように，(　) 内に適当な1語を補いなさい。

1. He is (　　) about people's manners.
　(彼は人の行儀にうるさい)
2. His (　　) had a baby boy.
　(彼に男の子が生まれた)
3. He has a hard time (　　) for a family of five.
　(彼が家族5人を食べさせていくのは大変なことだ)
4. He is so busy that he can't even take Sundays (　　).
　(彼は忙しくて日曜日でも休むことができない)
5. She and her husband are living separately because he was (　　).
　(彼女は夫の転勤で別れて暮らしている)
6. What is it (　　) me that you don't like?
　(僕のどこが気に入らないんだ)

7. The new teacher is (　　) from college.
   (新任の先生は大学出たての方です)
8. On such a small income it's impossible to get (　　).
   (そんなわずかな収入では暮らしてゆけない)
9. She remained single (　　) her life.
   (彼女は一生独身で通した)
10. We're (　　) friendly terms with our neighbors.
    (近所の人と親しくおつきあいしている)

■[考え方]　1. hard to please と同義の形容詞.　2. 結婚し, 子を生むのは母親.　3.「扶養する」は support＝provide for　4.「非番で」の意の副詞.「休暇を3日とる」を take three days off という.　5.「転勤させられる」は受動態.　6.「彼女にはどことなく気品がある」は, There is something noble *about* her. というが.　7.「新入生」の freshman を参考に.　8.「暮らす」の意の動詞句.　9.「一生」は through life ともいう.　10. (　　) friendly terms with は「親しい間柄」の意の熟語. 前置詞を入れる

■[解答]　1. particular [fastidious]　2. wife　3. providing　4. off　5. transferred　6. about　7. fresh　8. by [along]　9. all　10. on

【II】　次の日本文の中の「遅れる」という語句に同じ表現を使わず英訳しなさい.
1. この時計は5分遅れている.
2. 終電車に乗り遅れるとは, なんとも不注意だったね.
3. 夕食に遅れないようにもどりなさい.
4. 彼は約束の時間に20分遅れた.
5. 列車は雪で遅れている.

■[考え方]　1.「進んでいる」は be fast.「遅れている」は?　2.「乗り遅れる」は, miss the train か, または fail to catch the train. 3.「遅れない」は「間に合うように」と解し, in time for を用いる. 4.「約束の時間」は the appointment だけでよい. 5.「雪で」は「雪のため」と句にする.「遅れている」は,「予定より遅れて運行している」と解し, run behind schedule. 反対は, run on schedule

■[解 答] 1. This watch [clock] is five minutes slow. 2. How careless of you to miss the last train! 3. Get back in time for dinner. 4. He was twenty minutes late for the appointment. 5. The trains are running behind schedule because of the snow.

【III】 次の各文の空所に日本文と同じ意味になるよう時間を表わす1語を補いなさい.
1. This novel can easily be read (　　) three hours.
 (この小説は3時間もあれば読める)
2. I stayed up (　　) eleven o'clock last night.
 (昨夜は11時まで起きていた)
3. I have to hand in my paper (　　) tomorrow.
 (明日までにレポートを提出しなければならない)
4. There is plenty of time (　　) your departure.
 (出発まで時間はたっぷりある)
5. He got to the station seconds (　　) the train had left.
 (駅に着くのがひと足遅く, 電車は出たあとだった)

■[考え方] 1.「3時間もあれば」は,「3時間のうちに」の意で, 期間の経過を示す前置詞. 2.「11時まで」という継続を表わす前置詞. 3. hand in という動詞句は, 明日までに提出を完了することを表わす. 4.「出発する前に」という意味の前置詞. 5.「ひと足遅く, 電車は出たあと…」は,「電車が出たあと, 数秒のところで」と解し,「あと」の意の接続詞

■[解 答] 1. in　2. till [until]　3. by　4. before　5. after

Let's Memorize

1. 彼は人生に高遠な理想を抱いている．

   He has lofty ideals in life.

2. 彼女は大変家庭に恵まれている．

   She is blessed with a very happy home life.

3. 彼は几帳面で約束の時間に遅れたことがない．

   He is always quite punctual and has never been late for an appointment.

4. 叔父は何をするにも楽観的だ．

   My uncle is optimistic about whatever he does.

5. 彼女の内気な性格は大人になってからも直らなかった．

   She never got over her shyness even after she grew up.

6. 彼には男らしいところがない．

   There is nothing manly about him.

7. 私たちの先生は自分に厳しく，人に寛大だ．

   Our teacher is strict with himself, but tolerant of others.

8. 私の収入では，家族5人が暮らしていくのがたいへん困難です．

   On my income, it's very difficult to support my family of five.

9. 物価が上がって，生活が年々苦しくなるばかりです．

   Prices are rising, and life is getting harder and harder every year.

10. 新しい家に引っ越して，通勤時間が倍かかるように

    Now that I've moved into my new house, it takes me

なった.

11. できれば今日中に，これを仕上げていただきたい.

12. 夜ふかしは翌日の仕事のさまたげになる.

13. 彼女は歩き方まで母親に似ている.

14. 彼女はまずしい人たちのために一生をささげようと決心した.

15. 失敗は成功のもとである.

twice the time to commute to work.

If possible, I would like to have this done by the end of the day.

Staying up late at night will interfere with your work the next day.

She really takes after her mother, even in the way she walks.

She made up her mind to devote her life to helping poor people.

You learn from your mistakes.

Exercises

―〈例題 1〉―
長い休みの前にあれこれ計画を立てて実行を試みるが，休みが終わると何もやっていないことがしばしばある.

■[語 句]　「計画を立てる」make plans /「実行する」execute, carry out, put...into practice [action]

■[考え方]　「あれこれ計画を立てて」をやさしく「たくさんの計画を立てる」くらいに訳してもいいだろう.「休みが終わると」は when the vacation is over か，句にして at the end of the vacation とも表現できる.「何もやっていない」は，結果を示す不定詞を用い，only to find...that ～，または，「結局は，

しばしば，計画の大部分は実行しないままとなる」と解し，end up leaving it unexecuted という動詞型も考えられる．

〈解　答　例〉

(i)　Before a long vacation I always make a lot of plans and try to put them into action, only to find that I have done nothing at the end of the vacation.

(ii)　I always try to carry out this plan or that made in advance before the long vacation, but often end up leaving it unexecuted when the vacation is over.

☆

――〈例題 2〉――
　東京周辺で留学している外国人学生の8割近くのものは，円高のため，収入内で生活をやりくりするのが非常に困難で，生活費をまかなうため，彼らは食費を切りつめたり，アルバイトをふやしたりしている．

■[語句]　「東京周辺」in Tokyo and its suburbs, in and around Tokyo /「8割」80 percent /「円高」the strong yen /「収入内で…やりくりする」make (both) ends meet, live within one's income /「生活費をまかなう」pay [meet] one's living expenses /「食費を切りつめる」cut food expenses /「アルバイトをふやす」increase part-time work [jobs]

■[考え方]　「…外国人学生の8割近くが…生活をやりくりするのが困難で」を独立させ，「～が困難である」と区切ってしまうのがよい．ここに，have a lot of difficulty (in) ~ing の頻出構文を用いる．または，「困難である」を形容詞にし，find it so difficult to ~ that… と so ~ that… の相関接続詞を用い，後半の部分を that 節にするのもよい．「アルバイトをふやす」は，「前よりも多くのアルバイトをする」と考える．

⟨解　答　例⟩

(i)　About eighty percent of the foreign students living in and around Tokyo have a lot of difficulty making ends meet because of the strong yen. In order to pay their living expenses they have to cut food expenses or do more part-time jobs than they used to.

(ii)　Nearly 80 percent of the foreign students studying in and near Tokyo find it so difficult to make ends meet due to the strong yen that they have to reduce food expenses and increase part-time work in order to cope with their living expenses.

☆

⟨例題 3⟩

彼は貧しさにもめげない努力家で，子供たちには，自分の子供の頃より良い生活をさせてやりたいと思っていた．彼は働きながら大学を出て技術者になった．

■[語句]　「努力家」a hard worker /「働きながら大学を出る」work one's way through college

■[考え方]　「貧しさにもめげない努力家で」は，「貧しいけれども努力家であった」と訳す．「子供たちには…より良い生活をさせてやりたい」は，「自分の子供時代よりも裕福にさせたい」とし，want+目的語+to be more comfortably off than he used to be in his childhood とするか，「子供たちによい生活を与えたい」と解し，hope to provide+目的語+with a better life than he had when he was a child とする．最後の文の，「大学を出て」は，「大学を出たあとで」と考えればよい．

⟨解　答　例⟩

(i)　He was very poor, but hard working. He wanted his children to be more comfortably off than he used to be in his childhood. He became an engineer after working his way through college.

(ii) Although he was very poor, he was a hard worker, and hoped to provide his children with a better life than he had when he was a child. After working his way through college, he proved himself to be an engineer.

☆

――〈例題 4〉――
　僕がいちばん感謝するのは，父上が何も隠さず率直に僕に話してくださったことです．僕は父上の手紙のひとつひとつから，人間がどう生きるかを学ぶことができました．

■[語 句]　「感謝する」thank (you) for, be grateful for
■[考え方]　「父上」とあるので，息子が父親にあてた手紙文であることに注意する．「僕がいちばん感謝するのは...話してくださった」は，「僕は，お父さんが僕に隠しだてがなかったことにいちばん心から感謝する」とし，thank＋目的語＋for ～ の文型を用いる．または，「感謝していることは，父上が何も隠さず本当のことを僕に話してくれたことだ」と訳してもよい．第2文は，「手紙のひとつひとつから，僕は人生の意味を学ぶことができた」とするか，「父上の手紙は，人生とは何かを僕が学ぶことを可能にした」とし，S＋make＋it＋possible (for me)＋to 不定詞の文型を用いるとよい．

〈解　答　例〉

(i) I thank you, Father, most cordially for having been quite frank with me. I have been able to learn the meaning of life from each one of your letters.

(ii) What I am most grateful for is that you, Father, told me the truth without hiding anything. Each one of your letters has made it possible for me to learn what life is all about.

第 5 章
交通・旅行

Check & Check

☐ この通りは交通量が多い ⇨ This street has a lot of traffic.
  ▶The traffic is heavy [busy] on this street. または, There is a lot of traffic on this street. など同義の表現

☐ 列車に乗る ⇨ take [get on] a train

☐ 列車から降りる ⇨ leave [get off] a train

☐ 列車に間に合う ⇨ catch [be in time for] a train

☐ 7時の電車に乗り遅れる ⇨ miss the seven o'clock train

☐ 車で出勤する ⇨ drive to work
  ▶「(電車などで)通勤する」⇨ commute to work /「電車で通学する」⇨ go to school by train, take a train to school /「徒歩で通学する」⇨ walk to school

第5章　交通・旅行

□ひと駅乗り越す ⇨ ride past one station
　▶「自分の駅を乗り越す」⇨ miss one's station

□広島へ行く途中，大阪で下車する ⇨ stop over at Osaka on the way to Hiroshima

□列車はすし詰めだった ⇨ The train was jam-packed.
　▶「混んでいる」は，主語が (a)「列車」(b)「通り」(c)「交通」などにより，次のように異なる．
　(a)　The train is crowded [full, (jam-)packed].
　(b)　The street is busy [crowded, congested].
　(c)　The traffic is heavy [busy, congested].

□交通渋滞 ⇨ traffic congestion, a traffic jam
　▶congestion は無冠詞．jam は冠詞をつける
　▶「その市の交通の混雑を緩和する」⇨ relieve the city's traffic congestion

□交通を整理する ⇨ control (the) traffic

□大雪のため，何時間も交通が途絶した ⇨ Heavy snow held up [stopped] traffic for hours.
　▶受動態：Traffic was held up by the heavy snow.
　▶この表現では，traffic は無冠詞が普通

□駅まで車に乗せてくれてありがとう ⇨ It's nice of you to give me a ride [a lift] [drive me] to the station.
　▶give me a ride [a lift] は，不定冠詞 a をつける

□今度の日曜日にドライブに行かないか ⇨ How about going for a drive next Sunday?
　▶How about ～？は「提案，勧誘」などに用いる．Why not go for a ride? も同義．a ride も a drive も名詞表現で，不定冠詞 a をつける

□北海道に5泊6日の旅行をする ⇨ take a six-day [six days']

trip to Hokkaido
▶「ヨーロッパ旅行に出かける」⇨ go on a trip to Europe
▶a tour を用いると，make [take] a tour of Europe か go on a tour of Europe となる

☐陸の旅行が好きだ ⇨ I am fond of [like] traveling by land.
▶I like a travel by land. はよくない

☐旅行ほど楽しいものはない ⇨ Nothing is as pleasant as traveling.

☐旅行代理店 ⇨ travel agency [travel bureau]
▶「旅行案内業者」⇨ a travel agent

☐日光に日帰り旅行をいっしょにしませんか ⇨ What do you say to going on a one-day trip to Nikko with me?
▶What do you say to のあとは，名詞または動名詞形を用い，相手の意志を問う形

☐私は10時発のシカゴ行きの飛行機に乗った ⇨ I took the 10 o'clock plane to Chicago.

☐離陸[着陸]する ⇨ take off [land]

☐パリへの空の旅は快適でしたか ⇨ Did you have a comfortable [good] flight to Paris?
▶この表現では，不定冠詞 a をつけ，形容詞を伴う

☐彼はロンドンに短時間滞在した後，空路日本に帰還した ⇨ He flew back to Japan after a short stay in London.

☐午後4時発ロス行きの飛行機に予約した ⇨ I had a reservation [reservations] for the four p.m. flight to Los Angeles.
▶「予約」の意の reservation は，不定冠詞 a をつけるか，無冠詞で複数形

第5章　交通・旅行

□そのホテルにひと部屋を予約した ⇨ I made a reservation [reservations] for a room at the hotel.

□飛行機は安全だが，運賃が高い ⇨ Flying is safe but expensive.

□この超特急は乗り心地がよい ⇨ This bullet train is comfortable to ride in.
　▶「新幹線」の場合は，This Shinkansen train ともいう

□世界一周の旅行をする ⇨ travel round the world
　▶「海外へ旅行する」⇨ travel abroad [to a foreign country] /「ヨーロッパを広く旅行する」⇨ travel widely in Europe /「陸路[水路，鉄道]で旅行する」⇨ travel by land [water, train] /「気晴らしのために旅行する」⇨ travel for one's pleasure

□徒歩旅行 ⇨ a walking trip, a journey on foot
　▶「修学旅行」⇨ a school excursion /「視察旅行」⇨ an inspection tour /「探検旅行」⇨ an expedition /「宇宙旅行」⇨ a journey in (outer) space
　▶スポーツとして，食料・キャンプ用具等を背負って山野を歩くことを backpacking という． *cf.* go backpacking

□パナマ運河経由の船でニューヨークへ行く ⇨ sail for [to] New York by way of [via] the Panama Canal

□スイスに観光に行く ⇨ go sightseeing *in* Switzerland
　▶go *to* Switzerland to do the sights. この表現も同義であるが，前置詞が違うことに注意

□観光[行楽]地 ⇨ a tourist [holiday] resort
　▶京都・奈良など「観光の名所」は a tourist spot という

□景勝の地 ⇨ a beauty [scenic] spot, a place of scenic interest

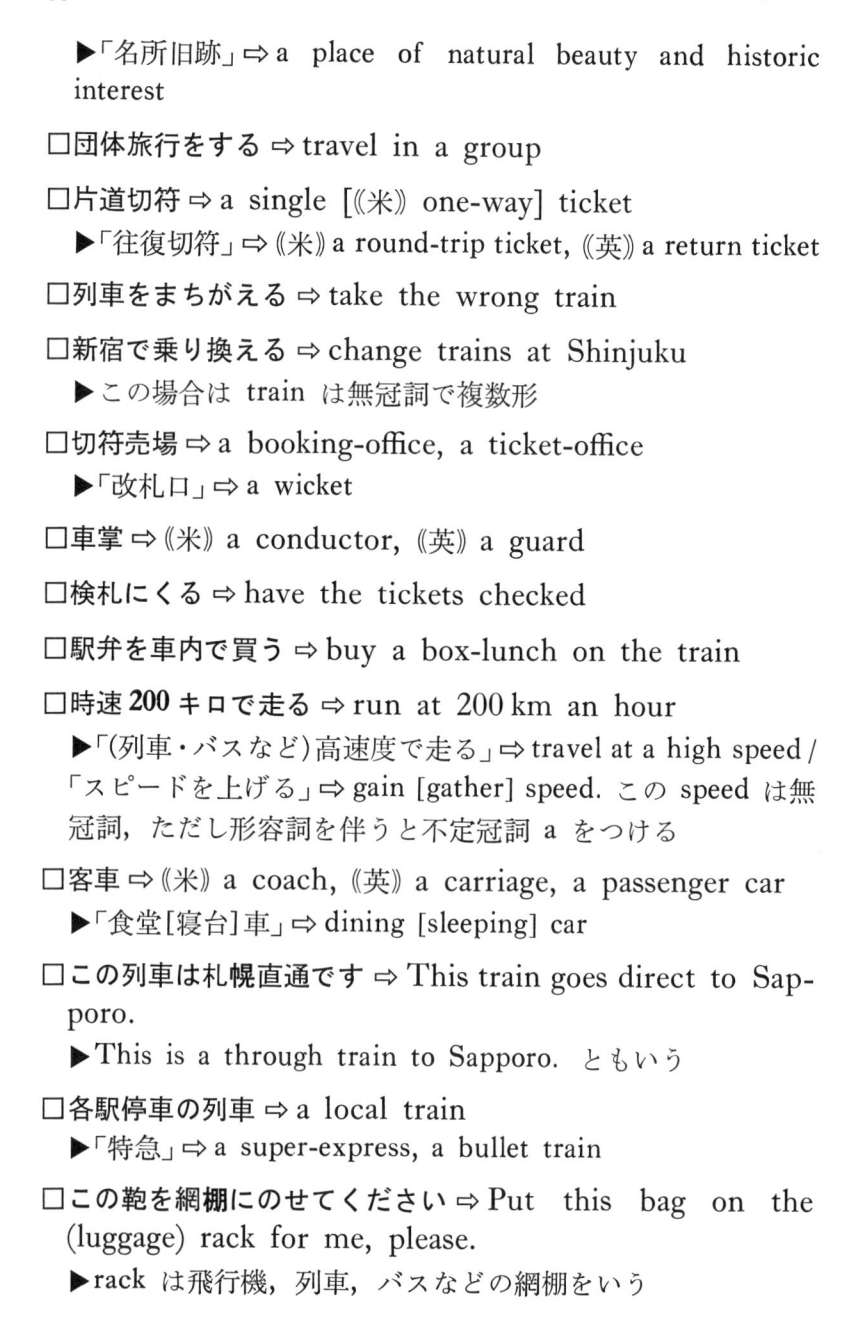

▶「名所旧跡」⇨ a place of natural beauty and historic interest

□団体旅行をする ⇨ travel in a group

□片道切符 ⇨ a single [《米》one-way] ticket
　▶「往復切符」⇨《米》a round-trip ticket, 《英》a return ticket

□列車をまちがえる ⇨ take the wrong train

□新宿で乗り換える ⇨ change trains at Shinjuku
　▶この場合は train は無冠詞で複数形

□切符売場 ⇨ a booking-office, a ticket-office
　▶「改札口」⇨ a wicket

□車掌 ⇨《米》a conductor,《英》a guard

□検札にくる ⇨ have the tickets checked

□駅弁を車内で買う ⇨ buy a box-lunch on the train

□時速200キロで走る ⇨ run at 200 km an hour
　▶「(列車・バスなど)高速度で走る」⇨ travel at a high speed /「スピードを上げる」⇨ gain [gather] speed. この speed は無冠詞, ただし形容詞を伴うと不定冠詞 a をつける

□客車 ⇨《米》a coach,《英》a carriage, a passenger car
　▶「食堂[寝台]車」⇨ dining [sleeping] car

□この列車は札幌直通です ⇨ This train goes direct to Sapporo.
　▶This is a through train to Sapporo. ともいう

□各駅停車の列車 ⇨ a local train
　▶「特急」⇨ a super-express, a bullet train

□この鞄を網棚にのせてください ⇨ Put this bag on the (luggage) rack for me, please.
　▶rack は飛行機, 列車, バスなどの網棚をいう

第5章　交通・旅行

☐ 電車で婦人に席をゆずる ⇨ give [offer] one's seat to a woman on a train
　▶「婦人が座れるよう席をあける」⇨ make room for a woman /「この席はふさがっていますか」⇨ Is this seat taken?

☐ ベルトをしめる[はずす] ⇨ fasten [unfasten] the seat belt

☐ アメリカ行きの船 ⇨ a ship bound for the United States
　▶「豪華船」⇨ a luxury liner /「出港する」⇨ leave port, set sail /「入港する」⇨ enter port /「寄港する」⇨ call at a port

☐ ヨットで太平洋を横断する ⇨ cross the Pacific aboard a sail(ing) boat
　▶ヨット (a yacht) は遊覧用のモーターつきの豪華快走船のこと

☐ ジャンボ・ジェット機 ⇨ a jumbo jet
　▶「超音速ジェット機」⇨ a supersonic jet

☐ 時差ボケ ⇨ jet lag
　▶ jet fatigue ともいう

☐ スチュワーデス ⇨ a stewardess
　▶性別の明示を避けて a flight attendant ともいう

☐ ガイドがニューヨーク市を案内してくれた ⇨ The tour guide showed us around New York City.

☐ 飛行機に乗り込む ⇨ board a plane
　▶ board (=get on) は飛行機，バス，列車，船などに乗り込むこと．「車に乗り込む」は get *into* a car

☐ エンジンの故障でヘリコプターは不時着した ⇨ Because of engine troubles, the helicopter made a forced landing.
　▶「無事着陸をする」⇨ make a safe landing

☐ 空港からホテルにバスの便がある ⇨ There is a bus service available from the airport to the hotel.

☐ホテルに泊まる手続きをする ⇨ check in at a hotel
　▶check in は「(ホテルや空港で)所定の手続き用紙に記名する」こと

☐ホテルに1泊する ⇨ stay overnight at a hotel

☐客はポーターにチップを与えた ⇨ The guest gave the porter a tip.

☐(勘定を払って)ホテルを出る ⇨ check out
　▶check out で「ホテルで勘定を支払って出る」の意

☐この旅行者用小切手はここで現金化できますか ⇨ Can I cash this traveler's check [《英》cheque] here?

☐南極大陸の探検旅行に出かける ⇨ go on an expedition to the Antarctic Continent
　▶南極大陸を Antarctica と大文字にして無冠詞でいう. Antarctic は Arctic (北極の)からの逆成語

☐親善の目的でヨーロッパの3ヵ国を歴訪する ⇨ visit three European countries for [on] a goodwill tour

☐花子はよくお母さんのお使いに行きます ⇨ Hanako often goes on an errand for her mother.
　▶run an errand も同義

☐公用で渡航する ⇨ go abroad on official business
　▶「用事で来たのであって, 遊びではない」⇨ I'm here on business, not for pleasure.

☐母はよく買物に下町へ私を連れて行った ⇨ My mother often took me downtown on a shopping trip.
　▶「父は私を志賀高原のスキー場に連れて行ってくれた」⇨ My father took me skiing at Shiga Heights.

☐東京の公共輸送機関は改善されつつある ⇨ Tokyo's public

transport system has been improving.
- □高速道路 ⇨ an expressway
  - ▶東名高速道路 ⇨ the Tokyo-Nagoya Expressway
- □高架を走る列車 ⇨ an elevated train
  - ▶米口語で an L train という
- □地下鉄で行く ⇨ go by subway
  - ▶《英》は go by underground [tube] という。「地下鉄に乗る」⇨ take the subway, go on the underground

Let's Try

【Ⅰ】 次の各英文の（　　）内に下の日本文の意味になるように適語を1つ入れなさい。

1. My house is within a ten minutes' bus (　　) of the station.
   (私の家は駅から10分ぐらいバスに乗ればいいのです)
2. Hand luggage to be taken on (　　) the plane is limited to one piece.
   (機内持ち込みの手荷物は1個だけに制限されています)
3. His plane arrived at Narita twenty minutes (　　) schedule.
   (彼の乗っている飛行機は予定より20分遅れて成田に着いた)
4. He was (　　) on a business trip and wasn't in Tokyo that day.
   (彼はその日は出張で東京にいなかった)
5. I'm planning to take some time (　　) and go on a trip.
   (今度，暇をもらって旅行に行こうと思っている)
6. When I was in elementary school, I used to walk

a long way to and (　　) school.
（小学生の頃，学校までの長い道のりを歩いて通ったものだ）

7. He went to the trouble of drawing me a map of (　　) to get there.
（彼はそこへ行く地図をわざわざかいてくれた）

■[考え方] **1.**「乗る」意の名詞形． **2.** on (　　)＝aboard で「(船，列車，飛行機など)の中に」の意． **3.**「予定通りに」は on schedule.「遅れて」もこれをヒントに考える． **4.** 短時間の不在は，out (＝not at home) だが，やや長期の旅行で家にいない場合には，(　　) from home という． **5.**「暇をもらう」は，「仕事から離れて休暇をとる」と考える．「非番」は I am off duty. という **6.**「学校へ行く途中」は on the way to school というが，「行き帰り」は？ **7.**「そこへ行く方法」の意になる疑問詞

■[解　答] **1.** ride　**2.** board　**3.** behind　**4.** away　**5.** off　**6.** from　**7.** how

【II】　次に与えられている単語を並べ換え，下の日本文の意味になるようにしなさい．ただし，1語が不足している．

1. two minutes, nine o'clock, he, express, the, missed
（彼は9時発の急行に2分のところで乗り遅れた）

2. area, I, not, this, am, familiar
（私はこの辺の地理に暗い）

3. cherry trees, place, its, is, famous, this
（ここは桜の名所として名高いところです）

4. what, that plane, tell, arrive, please, time, me
（その飛行機の到着時間を教えてください）

5. leaves, there, lose, no, the, to, time, is, train
（列車の出発まであまり時間がない）

第5章　交通・旅行

■[考え方]　1.「2分のところで」の差を表わす前置詞は？　2.「暗い」は,「よく知らない」とする．　3.「名高い」は原因・理由を表わす前置詞で．　4.「到着時間」は未来時制を用い,名詞節で表わす．　5.「列車の出発まえは,ぐずぐずしている時間がない」とする

■[解答]　(下線語は補った語を示す) 1. He missed the nine o'clock express <u>by</u> two minutes.　2. I am not familiar <u>with</u> this area.　3. This place is famous <u>for</u> its cherry trees.　4. Please tell me what time that plane <u>will</u> arrive.　5. There is no time to lose <u>before</u> the train leaves.

【III】　次の日本文を英語に直しなさい．
1. 先週の日曜日はドライブに行き,楽しかった．
2. ここから,その大学まで車で20分以上かかる．
3. 新幹線のため,君たちはそこへは日帰りができるようになった．
4. うちの娘はヨーロッパ旅行のためお金をためている．
5. 警官は交通信号を無視した子どもをしかった．

■[考え方]　1.「ドライブに行く」go for a drive /「楽しかった」enjoy oneself または have a good time を用いる．　2.「車で」を「車で行く」と解し,go by car または drive とする．　3.「新幹線」を主語にし,make it possible to ～ の文型で．　4.「お金をためる」save up　5.「交通信号を無視する」ignore the traffic signal /「しかる」scold

■[解答]　1. We went for a drive and had a good time last Sunday.　2. It takes me more than twenty minutes to drive from here to the college.　3. The Shinkansen trains have made it possible for you to get there and back in a day.　4. My daughter is saving up for a trip to Europe.　5. The policeman scolded the child for ignoring the traffic signal.

Let's Memorize

1. 今朝は交通渋滞に巻き込まれた．

    I got caught in a traffic jam this morning.

2. バスがなければ，そこに行くには歩くよりしかたがない．

    If there's no bus, there's no other way to get there but to walk.

3. 新幹線でなら，そこへは日帰りすることもできる．

    If you take the Shinkansen train, you can even get there and back the same day.

4. 地下鉄ができて，交通の便が良くなった．

    It has become much easier to travel since the subway opened.

5. バスがなかなか来ない．

    The bus is a long time (in) coming.

6. 若いドライバーは交通法規を無視することが多い．

    Young drivers often ignore traffic regulations.

7. 今年は飲酒運転による交通事故が増えている．

    The number of accidents because of drunk(en) driving has increased this year.

8. 東京から札幌まで飛行機で約１時間半です．

    It takes about an hour and a half to fly from Tokyo to Sapporo.

9. 初めての外国旅行なので少し不安です．

    I'm a little uneasy since this is my first trip abroad.

10. 彼女は毎月カナダ旅行の費用を積み立てている．

    She is putting aside some money every month for her trip to Canada.

11. 飛行機に乗るのが怖くて，まだ海外旅行をしていない．	I'm afraid of flying, so I still haven't traveled overseas.
12. 3日間の休暇をとって旅行に出た．	I took three days off from work and went on a trip.
13. 気分転換に伊豆へ旅行でもしたら．	Why don't you take a trip to the Izu Peninsula just for a change of pace?
14. 旅行が取りやめになったので，ホテルの予約を取り消した．	The trip fell through, so I canceled the hotel reservations.
15. 健康のために，車に乗らずに歩くように心がけている．	For health reasons I'm trying to walk more and drive less.

Exercises

〈例題 1〉

私は6月の終わり頃，英国へ旅行し2ヵ月間滞在することに決めました．冬にアルバイトをしながら稼いだお金で足りればいいんですが．

■[語句]「6月の終わり頃」about the end of June, late in June /「決める」make up one's mind to ～ /「アルバイトする」do [work at] a part-time job, work part-time /「足りる」do, be enough

■[考え方]「～へ旅行し...滞在することに決めました」の時制は，現在完了を用い，旅行の計画が現在も継続していることを表わす．第2文を，「冬にアルバイトして蓄えた金が足りることを願う」と解し，I hope (that) S+V の構文を用いる．hope の導く that 節は，願望を表わす未来時制にするのが普通

〈解　答　例〉

(i)　I have decided to take a trip to England late in June and stay there for two months. I hope the money I saved by working at a part-time job in the winter will be enough.

(ii)　I have made up my mind to travel to England about the end of June, with a view to staying there for a couple of months. I expect the money I laid aside working part-time in the winter will do.

☆

〈例題 2〉

　一昨日，東京駅からタクシーに乗ったが，ちょうど夕方の交通ラッシュが始まっていて，ずいぶん時間がかかってしまった．会に遅れるのではないかと気が気でなかったが，かろうじて間に合った．

■[語 句]　「夕方の交通ラッシュ」the evening rush hour, the evening rush-hour traffic /「かろうじて」just, barely, somehow
■[考え方]　「交通ラッシュが始まっていて」は，「タクシーに乗った」ときより前の時制，すなわち，過去完了時制を用いる．「会に遅れる...気が気でなかった」は，I was afraid [worried] that ~ might [would] の構文が適切．「かろうじて間に合う」は「なんとか時間に間に合った」と訳す

〈解　答　例〉

(i)　The day before yesterday I took a taxi at Tokyo Station. The evening rush hour had already begun, so it took me a very long time. I was afraid that I would be late for the meeting, but I somehow managed to arrive in time.

(ii) When I took a taxicab at Tokyo Station the day before yesterday, it took a lot of time, just because the evening rush-hour traffic had already started. I was really worried that I would be late for the meeting, but I just managed to make it.

☆

──〈例題 3〉──
　バスが出発して間もなく，隣の席に，私とちょうど同じ年頃の女子学生が乗り合わせてきました．彼女と話しだすと面白くて，運転手に告げられなかったら，乗り越しをしてしまっていたほどでした．

■［語　句］「私と同じ年頃の女子学生」a girl student (of) about my age /「乗り合わせる」happen to get on board /「乗り越す」ride past (one's stop)

■［考え方］「隣の席に...学生が乗り合わせた」は，「私と同じ年の女子学生が来て，隣に座った」とやさしい英語で表現する．「話しだすと面白く」は，「彼女と話しはじめると，彼女がとても話し相手として楽しいことが私にわかった」とするか，「ふたりとも会話をはじめた．すると私はその会話が楽しかったので...」と解し，such [so] ～ that... の相関接続詞を使うとよい．「運転手に(降りるところを)告げられなかったら，乗り越しをしてしまったろう」は，**仮定法過去完了形を用い，条件節は，had+P.P. にし，主節は might+have+P.P. を用いる．**

〈解　答　例〉

(i) Soon after the bus left, a girl student of about my age came and sat next to me. When I began to chat with her, I found she was such a pleasant girl to talk to that I might have ridden past my stop if the driver had not told me where to get off.

(ii) A little after my bus left, a female student just about my age happened to get aboard and take the seat next to mine. Both of us got into conversation, and I enjoyed myself talking with her so much that if the driver had not warned me, I might have missed my stop.

☆

──〈例題 4〉──
子供のときから汽車が好きで、当時は機関士になるのを理想にしていた．いまでもときどき、汽車に乗りたいばかりに旅行することがある．

■[語 句] 「機関士」engineer, engine driver /「理想」ambition, dream
■[考え方] 「子供のときから…好き」は、「子供のとき以来…ずっと好きである」と考え、接続詞に since を使い、「好き」の動詞を現在完了形で表わす．「当時は」以下の文は、過去形でよい．「乗りたいばかりに」は「ただそれが面白いから」とか、「汽車に乗るよりほかに何の考えもなく」くらいに訳す．

〈解　答　例〉

(i) I have been fond of trains since I was a child, and my dream in those days was to be an engineer. Even now I often travel by train simply for the fun of it.

(ii) I have been such a great lover of trains since my childhood that my ambition then was to grow up to be an engine driver. Even now I sometimes go on a trip, with no other intention than to take a train.

☆

第5章　交通・旅行

───〈例題 5〉───
昨年，私は約10ヵ月間ヨーロッパに滞在し，イタリアの南端から北欧諸国にかけて，ゆっくりと気ままに見物することができた．専門がヨーロッパの歴史であるため，一般の人々がめったに行かないような田舎の古い小都市や農村も訪ねる機会をもった．

■[語 句] 「気ままに」as I like [wish] /「専門」one's specialty
■[考え方] 　第一文は，「〜に滞在し，ゆっくり...見物して」のあとに「イタリアの南端から北欧諸国を旅しながら」と分詞形で続ける．「ゆっくりと...見物することができた」は，「少し時間をかけて見物する」と解し，spend some time (in) seeing the sights, または，take my time 〜ing などとする．「一般の人々がめったに行かない」は形容詞節にし，「小都市や農村」を修飾させる．

〈解　答　例〉

(i)　Last year I was able to stay in Europe about ten months and spend some time seeing the sights as I liked, traveling from the southern tip of Italy to the countries in northern Europe. Because my specialty is European history, I had a chance to go to many old towns and villages in the countryside where ordinary people seldom go.

(ii)　I was in Europe for ten months or so last year, and took my time traveling from the southern tip of Italy to the north of Europe, and seeing as many places as I wanted. Since I majored in European history, I had an opportunity of paying personal visits to such remote old towns and villages as ordinary tourists rarely visit.

第6章
社交・通信

Check & Check

☐今日の午後は来客がある ⇨ We're expecting company this afternoon.
　▶この company（来客）は単数形，無冠詞

☐ジムとメアリーはつき合っているが，結婚はしないと思う ⇨ Jim and Mary are keeping company, but I don't think they'll ever marry.
　▶この company（交際）も単数形，無冠詞

☐ジョンはつき合っておもしろい人物だ ⇨ John is good company.
　▶この company も無冠詞. good company＝a good person to be with「つき合っておもしろい人」

☐明日，彼がうちにいるかどうか電話して聞いてみよう ⇨ I'll

call him and ask if he will be (at) home tomorrow.
　▶call と phone は同義
□いつか遊びに来なさい ⇒ Come over and see us sometime.
　▶come over は「形式ばらない，短い訪問をする」の意
□人に手紙を書く ⇒ write (a letter) to a person
　▶He writes me a letter. も He writes to me. も同義
□トムはこの夏，来日すると手紙でいってきた ⇒ Tom wrote me that he'd be coming to Japan this summer.
　▶Tom wrote me to say that... も同義
□お手紙ありがとう ⇒ Thank you very much for your (kind) letter.
□長らくご無沙汰して申しわけありません ⇒ I hope you will forgive [excuse] me for not having written you for a long time.
　▶forgive, excuse はともに他動詞. Please accept my apologies for not writing for so long. も同義の表現
□君への手紙の返事が遅れてすいません ⇒ I'm sorry for being slow in answering your letter.
　▶この answer [=reply to] は他動詞
□ご返事をお待ちしています ⇒ I am looking forward to hearing from you.
　▶hear from=have a letter from の意
　▶look forward to のあとに不定詞を使うのは誤り
□その手紙の返事を出さずに放っておくのは失礼です ⇒ It's rude of you to leave the letter unanswered.
　▶leave＋目的語＋過去分詞の文型に注意
□ご家族の皆様はお元気ですか ⇒ How is everyone in your

family?
　▶同義の表現：How are you all getting along?

□われわれは10年来互いに文通している ⇨ We have corresponded with each other for ten years.
　▶correspond with は exchange letters regularly with と同義

□彼は筆無精だ ⇨ He is a poor [bad] letter writer.
　▶a bad correspondent も同義. correspondent は,「(新聞の)特派員」の意もある

□彼の消息をご存知なら，知らせてください ⇨ If you have heard anything of him, please let me know.
　▶hear of は hear about と同義

□アメリカのペンフレンドがいれば，すばらしい ⇨ How nice it is to have an American pen pal!
　▶a pen friend も同義

□シアトルにおいでの節は，ご連絡ください ⇨ Please get in touch with me when you come to Seattle.
　▶touch は「連絡」の意味では無冠詞. get in contact with someone も同義

□高校以来，彼女との連絡はない ⇨ I have been out of touch with her since high school.

□イギリス人の友人に夕食に招待された ⇨ I got [had, received] an invitation to dinner from an English friend of mine.
　▶動詞表現：I was invited to dinner by an English friend of mine.

□先約があって，彼の晩餐会への招待を断らざるを得なかった ⇨ I had to decline [refuse, turn down] his invitation

to dinner because of a previous engagement [appointment].
▶「招待を受ける」は accept one's invitation

□彼は父親の友人たちをその会でもてなす主人役をつとめた ⇨ He acted as host to his father's friends at the party.
▶この意味では host は無冠詞．cf.「オリンピックの主催国」を the host country for the Olympic Games という

□友人の田中氏をご紹介いたします ⇨ Let me introduce to you my friend Mr. Tanaka.
▶Meet Mr. Tanaka. も同義．なお，「自己紹介します」は Let me introduce myself : my name is... というのが普通

□今朝は郵便がたくさんきた ⇨ I got [had] a lot of mail this morning.
▶There was a lot of mail this morning. も用いられる

□航空便で手紙を出す ⇨ send a letter by air mail
▶「速達で」by special delivery [express] /「小包で」by parcel post

□書留にしてもらう ⇨ get [have] a letter registered

□この手紙に 62 円切手を貼るのを忘れるな ⇨ Don't forget to put a 62-yen stamp on this letter.

□この手紙を出してください．忙しくて外出できないから ⇨ Please post [mail] this letter for me, as I'm too busy to go out.

□この手紙の郵便料はいくらですか ⇨ What is the postage for [on] this letter?

□その結果を彼に電報する ⇨ telegraph [wire] him the results
▶「彼に電報を打つ」⇨ send a telegram [a wire, a cable]

to him

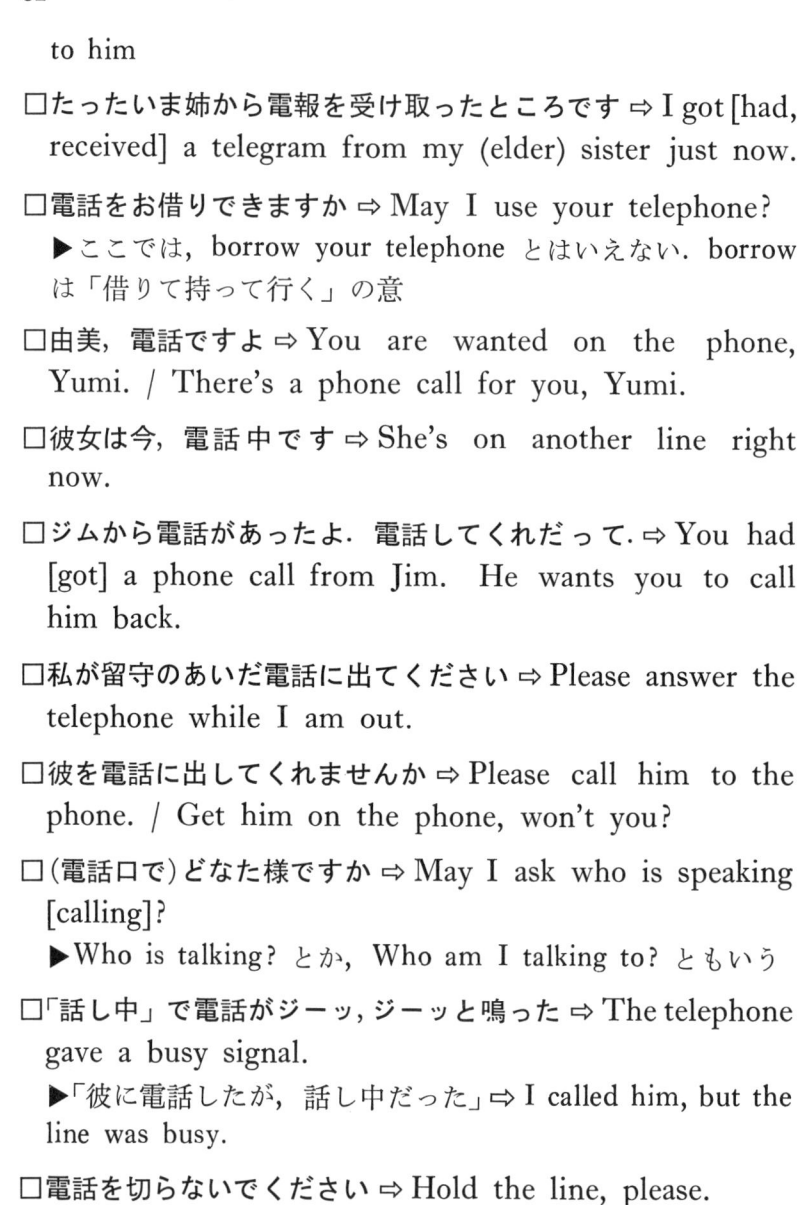

☐たったいま姉から電報を受け取ったところです ⇨ I got [had, received] a telegram from my (elder) sister just now.

☐電話をお借りできますか ⇨ May I use your telephone?
▶ここでは, borrow your telephone とはいえない. borrow は「借りて持って行く」の意

☐由美, 電話ですよ ⇨ You are wanted on the phone, Yumi. / There's a phone call for you, Yumi.

☐彼女は今, 電話中です ⇨ She's on another line right now.

☐ジムから電話があったよ. 電話してくれだって. ⇨ You had [got] a phone call from Jim. He wants you to call him back.

☐私が留守のあいだ電話に出てください ⇨ Please answer the telephone while I am out.

☐彼を電話に出してくれませんか ⇨ Please call him to the phone. / Get him on the phone, won't you?

☐(電話口で)どなた様ですか ⇨ May I ask who is speaking [calling]?
▶Who is talking? とか, Who am I talking to? ともいう

☐「話し中」で電話がジーッ, ジーッと鳴った ⇨ The telephone gave a busy signal.
▶「彼に電話したが, 話し中だった」⇨ I called him, but the line was busy.

☐電話を切らないでください ⇨ Hold the line, please.

☐電話を切る ⇨ hang up [ring off]
▶「彼女は腹をたてて, 私の(話し中に)電話を切った」⇨ She

was so angry that she hung up on me. *cf.*「電話を切らないでおく」⇨ hang on

□彼にすぐ電話をよこすようにと，彼の家族の人にことづけてきました ⇨ I left a message with his family for him to phone me right away.

□ウェストン氏は昼食で外出しておりますが，何かおことづけがございますか？ ⇨ Mr. Weston has gone out for lunch; may I take a message?

□お母さんに今夜遅くなるって電話したらどうですか ⇨ Why don't you call your mother and tell her that you'll be home late tonight?

□今夜電話をくれ ⇨ Give me a call this evening, will you?
　▶動詞表現：Call me this evening, will you?

□ロンドンに電話したいのですが ⇨ I want to make a (phone) call to London.

□返事は E メールでください ⇨ Please reply by e-mail. / Please e-mail (me) your answer.
　▶「E メールを送る」⇨ send an e-mail

□すべて電話ですます ⇨ take care of everything over [on] the telephone
　▶この take care of ~ は，「~を処理する」の意

□近日中にお宅へお伺いしたいと思いますが，いつお目にかかれますか，ご一報ください ⇨ I would like to call at your house one of these days. Please let me know when I can see you.
　▶call at＋家, call on＋人．いずれも，ある目的や用事で「訪問する」意

□このあたりに来たついでに，ジム君のところに立ち寄ろう ⇨ Let's drop in on Jim while we're in the neighborhood.
▶drop in on＋人 は，「予告なく，ぶらりと立ち寄る」の意. look in on＋人も同義

□「お願いがあるのですが」「いいですよ．もし私にできることでしたら」⇨ "May I ask a favor of you?" "Yes, if it's anything I can do."
▶"Will you do me a favor?" ともいう．この表現では，favor は不定冠詞 a とともに用いる

□父は用事があって明日横浜へ行きます ⇨ My father is going to Yokohama on business tomorrow.

□お茶を飲みながら話しましょう ⇨ Let's have a talk over a cup of tea.
▶この over は，「～しながら」の意

□お父さんによろしく ⇨《口語》Say hello to your father for me.
▶Please give my best regards to your father. はあらたまった表現
▶「父もよろしくと申しておりました」は，My father sends you his regards. という．この表現では，regards, respects, best wishes などが用いられ，必ず複数形

Let's Try

【I】 次の英文の空所に，以下に与えられている語を補い，文意を完全にしなさい．
1. I had a (　　) installed in my house yesterday.
2. I called Carol, but the (　　) was busy.
3. You can judge a person's character by the (　　) he keeps.

4. If you have a (　　), I'll be glad to talk it over with you.
5. I made an overseas phone (　　) to England.
6. Please give her my best (　　) if you get a chance to see her.

> visitors　wish　line　company　phone
> regards　problem　call

■[考え方]　1.「昨日，私の家に電話を引きました」　2.「キャロルに電話をかけたが話し中だった」　3.「つき合っている仲間を見ればその人柄がわかる」　4.「困った問題があれば，相談にのりましょう」　5.「イングランドに国際電話をかけた」　6.「彼女に会う機会があれば，よろしく伝えてください」
■[解答]　1. phone　2. line　3. company　4. problem　5. call　6. regards

【II】　次の各英文が，それぞれ下の日本文に相当する意味になるように，カッコ中に適当な1語を入れなさい．
1. He makes (　　) with people right away.
   (彼はだれとでもすぐ仲良くなる)
2. It's time (　　) (　　). We've had a very (　　) time this evening.
   (もうおいとましなければならない時間です．今晩は実に楽しかったです)
3. I have to apologize for not (　　) to you for a long time.
   (長い間ごぶさたして，申し訳ありません)
4. Nothing makes me so happy as (　　) from home.
   (家から手紙がくることほどうれしいことはない)
5. Have you written (　　) to your aunt yet, thank-

ing her for her invitation?
（叔母さんにご招待のお礼の手紙を出しましたか）
6. (　　) there were telephones, people often wrote letters.
（電話がなかった時代は人はよく手紙を書いた）
7. Telephones are now in widespread (　　) all over the country.
（電話は今では全国に普及している）
8. No matter how often I write to him, I hardly ever get back a (　　).
（いくら彼に手紙を書いても，なかなか返事がこない）
9. It was nice of you to invite me, but I'll have to (　　).
（せっかくのご招待だが，私は断らなければならない）
10. Don't poke your (　　) into other people's business.
（他人のことに口を出すな）

■[考え方] 1.「友だちになる」とする． 2.「立ち去る」の意を2語で． 3.「便りを書かなかった」とする．having written を1語で表わす． 4. news でもよいが，「便りがくる」を ～ing 形で． 5.「返事を書く」は, write (　　) と副詞を伴う． 6.「より前に」の意の接続詞を入れる． 7.「用いられている」は being used だが, in＋名詞形で表わす． 8.「返信」は answer か, reply か． 9.「断る」refuse と同義の語は？ 10.「他人のことに口を出す」という日本語に対し，英語では，「鼻をつき出す」という

■[解 答] 1. friends　2. to leave [go], good　3. writing　4. hearing　5. back　6. Before　7. use　8. reply　9. decline　10. nose

Let's Memorize

1. 昨日ばったり街で親友に出会った．

   Yesterday I ran [bumped] into a close friend of mine on the street.

2. 若い人と接しないと，時代に取り残されると思う．

   I'm afraid you will fall behind the times if you don't come into contact with young people.

3. ミックは早口なので聞き取れなかった．

   Mick talked so fast (that) I couldn't catch what he said.

4. 30分ほどお時間をさいていただけませんか．

   Would you mind sparing me thirty minutes of your time?

5. 手紙をもらったら，できるだけ早く返事を出すのが礼儀です．

   When you receive a letter, it's good form to answer it as soon as possible.

6. お話し中失礼ですが，あなたにお電話です．

   Excuse me for interrupting, but there's a phone call for you.

7. 電話番号が違っていますよ．

   You've got the wrong number.

8. 彼女が家に戻りしだい，あとで私に電話するようにお願いします．

   Would you ask her to call me back as soon as she gets home?

9. 彼はいつも他人のあらさがしをしたがる．

   He is always ready to find fault with other people.

10. 何の用でここへ来たの？

    What's brought you here?

11.	彼は恥ずかしがって，人前では彼女に話しかけられない.	He is too bashful to speak to her in front of others.
12.	遅くなったので，私は家まで彼女を送った.	It was late, so I saw her home.
13.	どういう訳か，彼女は彼とは気が合わない.	I don't know why, but she doesn't get along with him.
14.	なにか必要なら，ためらわず，聞いて欲しい.	Don't hesitate to ask if you need anything.
15.	新任の先生は冗談をとばして，私たちをよく笑わせる.	Our new teacher often cracks jokes and makes us laugh.

Exercises

─〈例題 1〉─
　私はきのうカナダ人の技師のスミス氏を訪ねました. 5年ぶりで会ったのですが，困ったことに，相手の言うことはわかりましたが，こちらの言うことをわからせるのが困難でした.

■[語 句]　「5年ぶり」for the first time in five years /「困ったことに」The trouble was..., I was annoyed... /「こちらの言うことをわからせる」make oneself understood

■[考え方]　「5年ぶりで会った」は，「5年間会ったことがなかった」と過去完了形か，「5年間で初めて会った」と過去形で表わす.「こちらの言うことをわからせる」は上記のほかに,「相手」を目的語にして，make him understand what I say とすることもできる

〈解　答　例〉

(i)　Yesterday I called on Mr. Smith, a Canadian engineer, whom I had not seen for five years. I was annoyed because I understood what he said, but it was difficult to make myself understood.

(ii) Yesterday I paid a visit to Mr. Smith, a Canadian engineer, whom I saw for the first time in five years. The trouble was that I understood what he said, but I had difficulty in making him understand what I was trying to say.

☆

―〈例題 2〉――――――――――
　私の知っている外国人でとても判読しにくい字を書く人がいる．あるときその人から，自分の字は読みにくいといわれるが，これからは手紙をタイプにしましょうかといってきた．私はこれまで通り手書きにしてくださいとお願いした．

■[語句]「自分の字」one's handwriting /「手紙をタイプする」type one's letter
■[考え方]「判読しにくい字を書く」は，「字が下手なので，読むのがむずかしい」と解する．「彼は字が下手です」は He has bad handwriting. という．handwriting は無冠詞．「自分の字は読みにくいといわれる」は，「読みにくいと世間の人がいう」と能動態にするか，受動態で表わせる．ただし，「あるときその人から」ではじまる部分は，直接話法と間接話法の2通りに英訳できる．直接話法で作文する方がやさしい．

〈 解　答　例 〉

(i) A foreigner I know has such bad handwriting that I find it hard to read. He once said in a letter, "People say my handwriting is hard to read. Shall I type my letters from now on?" I answered, "Please write by hand as before."

(ii) There is a foreigner I know whose handwriting is hard to read. He once asked in a letter if he should type his letters from then on because his handwriting was said to be hard to read. I asked him to continue writing by hand as he had always done.

☆

──〈例題 3〉──
　どんなに忙しくても，学生が少なくとも月に一度は故郷の父母に手紙を出すことは，よい習慣である．親は子供の動静がわかり，学業の進歩を知ることができるからである．

■[語句]　「習慣」a habit, a practice /「動静」doings /「学業」studies, scholarship

■[考え方]　「どんなに忙しくても」は however [no matter how]＋形容詞＋S＋V の譲歩構文を用いる．「学生が...よい習慣である」は It is a good practice for...to ~ の文型を用いる．「学生」は単数に，「親」は複数で書く．そうすれば，代名詞にしても混乱しない．「動静」は「子供がどのような暮らしをしているか」と言い換える．同じように，「学業の進歩」も節にして，「学業がどんなに進んでいるか」くらいに意訳する．最後の「できるからである」は無視する．「からである」という日本文にひかれ，Because と大文字ではじめ，独立させるのはこの場合よくない．

〈解　答　例〉

(i) It is a good practice for a student to write to his parents at home at least once a month, however busy he may be. His letter will tell them how he is getting along and also what progress he is making in his studies.

(ii) Writing home to parents at least once a month is a good habit for a student to form, no matter how hard he is studying. It will enable his parents to learn how he is getting on and also how hard he is working at his studies.

☆

――〈例題 4〉――
　日本人が外国人と英語で話すとき,「アイ・シー」「アイ・アンダースタンド」とさかんにやる. これは相手の意見に賛成という意味にとられがちである. しかし, 実は, これは会話を進行させるあいづちで, 相手の言い分に賛成しているわけではない.

■[語 句]「人の意見に賛成する」agree with a person's opinion, agree with a person /「会話を進行させる」keep the conversation going

■[考え方]「これは...意味にとられがちです」は this tends to be taken to mean... とする.「相手の意見に賛成」を, that 節にして,「あなたが外国人の意見に賛成している」とするか,「これらの言葉を聞いて, 外国人はあなたが同意していると思うであろう」と訳しやすい日本文に換える.「実は」は, the truth is... と挿入する.「これは...あいづちで」は,「これは会話を進行させるための応答 (responses) にすぎない」と考える. 最後の「相手の言い分に賛成しているわけではない」の中の「わけではない」は,「意味していない」とする. この場合の mean は他動詞で, 名詞かまたは that 節を従える.

〈 解　答　例 〉

(i) When speaking English with a foreigner, a Japanese says very often, " I see," or " I understand." This tends to be taken to mean that he agrees with the foreigner's opinion. The truth is, however, that this is nothing but the response a Japanese makes to keep the conversation going, and does not mean that he agrees.

(ii) A Japanese, when in conversation with a foreigner, says repeatedly, ' I see ' or ' I understand.' Hearing these expressions, the foreigner is likely to think that you are in agreement with him. In fact, however, they do not mean that you are of the same opinion; they are merely the responses you give, so that the conversation can go on smoothly.

☆

――〈例題 5〉――
電話というものは，ベルが鳴り出したら，何をしていようが，応対を余儀なくされる．だから，こちらから電話をかけるときも，相手に迷惑をかけないようにしている．それが電話のエチケットではないか．

■[語 句]「応対する」answer the phone /「電話をかける」make a phone call /「迷惑をかける」make oneself a nuisance to, annoy, bother

■[考え方]「電話...鳴り出したら」は，「いったん電話が鳴ると」と解し，Once を接続詞に用いる．「何をしていようが...余儀なくされる」は「そのとき，何をしていても，電話に出なければならない」(you have to answer the phone, even when you are doing something at that moment) とする．「こちらから電話をかけるとき」の「こちらから」は「私が...」と解する．「相手に迷惑をかけないようにしている」の「相手に」は，「私が電話している人に」と言えば，英文の意味がはっきりわかる．「電話のエチケット」は「電話するとき，これはエチケットです」と考えて，英訳する．

〈 解　答　例 〉

(i)　Once the telephone rings, you have to answer it, even when you are doing something at that moment. So, when I make a telephone call, I always try not to make myself a nuisance to the person I am calling. I believe that this is a matter of etiquette when you give a call.

(ii)　When the telephone starts ringing, you are obliged to answer it without a moment's delay, no matter what you are doing at the time. Therefore, when I make a phone call to someone, I always try not to cause inconvenience to him. I think it is a matter of etiquette to do so when telephoning.

第 7 章
風俗・習慣

Check & Check

☐ 英国民の風俗・習慣 ⇨ the manners and customs of the English people
　▶この manners は,「風習」の意で, 通例複数形. 複数形で,「行儀, 作法」の意にも用いられる. *cf.*「彼は行儀が悪い」⇨ He has no manners.

☐ 良い英語を使う習慣をつけなさい ⇨ You should form the habit of using good English.
　▶この表現の habit には定冠詞 the をつけ, あとに of 〜ing 形を続ける. habit のあとに, 不定詞を用いるのは誤り.
　▶form the habit は, 普通,「良い習慣をつける」の意

☐ おまえは宿題をほったらかす癖がついたね ⇨ You have fallen into the habit of leaving your homework undone.

第7章 風俗・習慣

▶fall into a habit は,「悪い習慣がつく」の意に普通用いられる．なお, get into a habit は, 善し悪しに関係なく, いずれの習慣にも用いられる

☐悪い癖をやめるのはむずかしい ⇨ It is difficult to break [get rid of, overcome, shake off] bad habits.

☐その習慣はいったん身につくと, なかなか抜けない ⇨ The habit is very hard to get out of when once acquired.
　▶habit は,「個人的習慣・癖」の意

☐国によって習慣が異なる ⇨ Customs vary [differ] from country to country.
　▶Each country has its own customs. ともいう
　▶custom は「世間一般的な習慣」の意

☐デパートは8時過ぎたら閉店するのが慣例だ ⇨ It's not the practice for department stores to stay open after eight o'clock.
　▶practice は「実行, 練習」の意から,「繰り返して行なう習慣」の意で, habit の意にも, custom の意にも用いられる

☐日本にいるときは, 日本の習慣に従うように努めなさい ⇨ When you are in Japan, you should try to follow Japanese customs.

☐この習慣は200年もこの地方で守られている ⇨ This custom has been kept up in this part of the country for two hundred years.
　▶「その土地独特のしきたり」⇨ local customs

☐この習慣の起源にさかのぼってみることは興味あることだ ⇨ It is interesting to trace this custom back to its origin.
　▶「昔からの習慣」⇨ a time-honored custom
　▶custom には, ①「得意先」と ②「税関」の意がある

① 「彼は得意先が多い[少ない]」⇨ He has a large [small] custom. (この custom は不定冠詞と形容詞を伴う)
② 「税関を通過するのに長い時間がかかった」⇨ It took me quite a long time to get through customs. (この意では, 通例, 無冠詞, 複数形)

□日本人には年末に人に贈り物をする習慣がある ⇨ It is customary with [for] the Japanese to give people gifts at the end of the year.
　▶customary は「慣習的に行なわれる」意

□彼が勤めに遅刻するのは, いつものことだ ⇨ It is usual with him to be late for work.
　▶usual は,「例によって, 相変わらず, いつもの」の意

□髪をなでるのが彼女の癖だ ⇨ It is habitual with her to pat her hair.
　▶habitual は「無意識に, どうしても出てくる癖の」の意

□彼は早寝早起きする習慣がある ⇨ He is in the habit of keeping early [good] hours.
　▶keep late [bad] hours は,「(帰宅, 就寝, 起床など)いつも遅い」の意. この表現では, hour は無冠詞, 複数形

□試験勉強で夜ふかしする ⇨ stay up (till) late at night studying for the examination
　▶「寝ずに起きて～する」は stay up ～ing を用いる. sit up ～ing も同義

□朝寝坊する ⇨ get up [rise] late, stay in bed late in the morning
　▶「いつもより朝寝する」⇨ get up later than usual /「朝寝坊の人」⇨ a late riser

□私は毎朝6時前に必ず起きるように心がけています ⇨ I make a point of getting up before six o'clock every morning.

第7章　風俗・習慣

▶不定詞を用いて，make it a point to ～ 不定詞も同義

□私は11時前に寝ることにしている ⇨ I make a practice of going to bed before eleven o'clock.
　▶普通, I usually go to bed before eleven o'clock. と現在時制で，習慣を表わす

□祖父は毎日朝食後, 散歩をすることにしている ⇨ My grandfather makes it a rule to take a walk after breakfast every day.
　▶普通, My grandfather usually takes a walk after breakfast every day. という

□こういう帽子が今はやっている[すたれている] ⇨ These hats are now in [out of] fashion.
　▶fashion は「衣服, 帽子, 髪」などの「流行」の意のみならず，「やり方, 態度, 振舞い」などの習慣的なものの「流行」にも用いられる

□今日の若者たちはスポーツカーをもつのがはやりだ ⇨ It's the fashion for young people today to have a sports car.

□ミニスカートがまたはやってきた ⇨ Miniskirts have come into fashion again.
　▶come into fashion の fashion は無冠詞

□長髪は間もなくすたれるだろう ⇨ Long hair will go out of fashion before long.

□流行を追う ⇨ follow the fashion
　▶fashion には定冠詞 the をつける

□正月の休暇にハワイに行くのがはやっている ⇨ It's fashionable to go to Hawaii for your New Year's holidays.
　▶fashionable は，服装ばかりでなく, 生活上の風習や行動に

ついても用いられる

- おいの大学入試の合格を祝った ⇨ We congratulated our nephew on having passed his college entrance examination.
    - ▶congratulate は「(〜について人に) 祝辞を述べる」の意. congratulate＋a person＋on＋名詞・動名詞の型が正用法
- 私たちは困難な役割における彼の成功に祝辞を呈した ⇨ We offered [sent] him our congratulations on his success in a difficult role.
    - ▶この表現では, congratulations と必ず複数形で
- 彼の80歳の誕生日を祝う ⇨ celebrate his eightieth birthday
    - ▶celebrate は, 祝典を挙げて「祝う」意. congratulate は人に対し, celebrate は行事に対して用いる
- 私たちはハローラン夫妻のために日曜日に晩餐会を催すつもりです ⇨ We are going to give a dinner for Mr. and Mrs. Halloran on Sunday.
    - ▶この a dinner は a dinner party の意. for＝in honor of
- 彼は私を晩餐会に招いた ⇨ He asked me to dinner.
    - ▶人をパーティーなどに実際, 招くとき, 相手に invite という動詞を用いない. そのときは, "Will you *come* to the party tomorrow?" などといい, 後になって, "I *invited* them to the party." などという
- クラス会を開く ⇨ hold a class meeting (在校生の場合), a class reunion (卒業生の場合)
    - ▶a reunion は親族, 親友, 卒業生などの再会の集りで, 可算名詞
- 彼はお客たちをくつろがせた ⇨ He put his visitors at their ease.

第7章　風俗・習慣

▶「くつろいでください」⇨ Please make yourself comfortable.

□彼は日本の習慣になじもうとしない ⇨ He won't adapt (himself) to Japanese customs.
　▶adapt は，自動詞にも他動詞にも用いられる．conform to ～ も同義

□和装の日本の少女たち ⇨ Japanese girls in [wearing] national costume(s)
　▶costume は「(ある階級，時代特有の)服装」をさすこともある．「仮装舞踏会」⇨ a costume ball

□彼がタバコを吸うのは癖で，楽しんではいない ⇨ He smokes out of habit, not for pleasure.
　▶「癖で」は，by habit ともいう

□彼はあごひげをはやし始めた ⇨ He began to grow a beard.
　▶「あごひげを生やしている」⇨ have [wear] a beard

□近ごろ，髪を長くしている女性がだんだん増えてきた ⇨ These days more and more women are wearing their hair long.
　▶これは S+V+O+C (形容詞) の文型

□挨拶(あいさつ)の仕方は国によってまちまちです ⇨ The way people greet each other differs [varies] from country to country.

□私はビルにクリスマスの挨拶状を出した ⇨ I sent Christmas greetings to Bill.
　▶「挨拶状」の意では複数形．「人に年賀状を出す」⇨ send the New Year's greetings to a person

□アメリカ人は紹介されると，よく握手をする ⇨ Americans often shake hands when they are introduced.
　▶この hand は，無冠詞，複数形

風俗・習慣

- □彼女は私にていねいにお辞儀した ⇨ She made [gave] a polite bow to me.
  - ▶動詞表現で，She bowed politely to me. とも書ける
- □日本人は，家にあがる前に靴を脱ぐ習慣があります ⇨ Japanese people have the custom of taking off their shoes before they enter their houses.
- □ナイフやフォークの代わりに，箸(はし)を使う ⇨ use chopsticks instead of a knife and fork
- □ソバを食べるとき音をたてる ⇨ make a sound when you eat buckwheat noodles [soba]
- □卵は半熟が好きです ⇨ I like eggs soft-boiled.
  - ▶「固茹で」は，hard-boiled. *cf.*「卵を目玉焼きにする」⇨ fry eggs sunny-side up
- □神社に初詣でする ⇨ visit [pay a visit to] a shrine on New Year's Day
- □お年玉として5000円をその子にやる ⇨ give 5,000 yen as a New Year's gift to the child
- □彼は私とはずっと以前からのつき合いです ⇨ He has been on good terms with me.
  - ▶この term は，必ず複数形. on friendly terms with ともいう. このほか，on speaking terms (言葉を交わす間柄), on visiting terms (訪問し合う仲) などのように用いられる
- □人にステーキをおごる ⇨ treat a person to a steak
  - ▶「私がおごる番だ」⇨ It's my treat. この treat は名詞 /「一杯おごるよ」⇨ Let me buy you a drink. /「割り勘」⇨ a Dutch treat /「割り勘にする」⇨ go Dutch
- □祝日 ⇨ a national holiday

第7章　風俗・習慣

▶文化の日は学校が休みです ⇨ Culture Day is a school holiday.

Let's Try

【Ⅰ】 次の各英文が、それぞれ下の日本文に相当する意味になるように、カッコ中に適当な1語を入れなさい．

1. In many countries it is (　　) to give flowers to people who are sick.
   (多くの国では病気の人に花を贈るのがしきたりになっている)
2. My father has fallen (　　) the habit of drinking a glass of whisky before he goes to bed.
   (父は寝る前に、ウイスキーを一杯飲む癖がついてしまった)
3. He had (　　) in getting rid of the habit of smoking.
   (彼は喫煙の習慣をやめるのに苦労した)
4. They live on sociable (　　) with their neighbors.
   (彼らは隣人たちと親しくつき合って暮らしている)
5. Please accept my (　　) on your recovery from illness.
   (ご病気回復され、おめでとうございます)
6. It's become (　　) for housewives in Japan to take part in many cultural activities outside their homes.
   (日本では主婦たちが多くの文化活動に参加するのがはやっている)

■[考え方]　1.「しきたりになっている」は、custom の形容詞で表わす．　2.「癖がつく」は get into the habit of ともいう．

3.「苦労する」は have a hard time ~ing も用いられる. 4.「間柄」の意の名詞を考える. 5.「祝辞」の意の複数名詞. 6.「はやっている」は fashion の形容詞で表わす

■[解答] 1. customary 2. into 3. difficulty 4. terms 5. congratulations 6. fashionable

【II】 次の単語を並べ換え, 下の日本文の意味になるようにしなさい.
1. practicing, the morning, she, a point, the violin, in, makes, of
   (彼女は朝のうちにバイオリンのけいこを必ずするよう心がけている)
2. following, loses, the fashion, time, my daughter, in, no
   (私の娘はすぐ流行を追う)
3. his fingernails, habit, excited, he, when, has, biting, a, he, gets, of
   (彼は興奮すると指の爪をかむ癖がある)

■[考え方] 1.「必ず~するよう心がける」は, 不定詞を使えば, make it a point [a rule] to ~ ともいうが, 動名詞構文では? 2.「すぐ」は「機を失せずに」と解し, lose no time in ~ing の動詞型を用いる. 3.「~の癖がある」は, He has a habit of ~ing の構文を用いる

■[解答] 1. She makes a point of practicing the violin in the morning. 2. My daughter loses no time in following the fashion. 3. He has a habit of biting his fingernails when he gets excited.

Let's Memorize

1. 早起きの習慣をつけるのはよいことだ. | It is a good idea to form the habit of getting up early.

2. 食事しながら，新聞を読むのが父の癖です．	My father has a habit of reading the newspaper while eating.
3. 喫煙は，なかなか抜けられない習慣です．	Smoking isn't an easy habit to get out of.
4. 爪を緑色に塗るのがはやりだ．	There is a fashion for painting your nails green.
5. 彼が事業に成功したことを祝って，パーティーを開く計画をしている．	We are planning to give a party to celebrate his success in business.
6. 彼らは古い日本の風習に従って婚礼をあげた．	They held their wedding ceremony according to old Japanese customs.
7. 元旦に神社に参拝するのが日本人の習わしでした．	It was customary with the Japanese to pay a visit to a shrine on New Year's Day.
8. 近ごろは，モチをつく家が少ない．	These days fewer people pound rice to make homemade rice cake.
9. 日本では，厄払いとして節分に豆をまく習慣がある．	In Japan there is a custom of throwing beans on the last day of winter to drive out evil spirits.
10. 古くからの習慣が，今でも多くこの地方に存続している．	Many ancient customs still exist in this part of the country.
11. 地方の風習には，とても変わったものがある．	Some of the local customs are quite unusual.

12. 外国へ行くと習慣の違いがわかるものだ.

People often realize how different customs are when they go to a foreign country.

13. アメリカのような大きな国では，車なしで生活するのは不自由だ.

It is inconvenient to live without a car in a big country like America.

14. この本はインドの習俗を詳しく紹介している.

This book introduces the customs of India in great detail.

15. そのような風習は，この国だけにとどまらない.

Such customs are not limited to this country.

Exercises

─〈例題 1〉─
　日本人は流行を追うのに非常に熱心すぎるように思われる．日本人は，他の人たちがしているのと同じことができないと不幸だと思うのだろう．ところが，西欧諸国では，たいてい，人々は自分のしたいと思うとおりのことをし，他人がしていることには関心をもたない．

■[語　句]　「流行を追う」follow the fashion /「熱心すぎる」have a passion for /「関心をもたない」do not show any interest in

■[考え方]　「非常に熱心すぎる」は単に「大好き」とか「愛する」とする．「人々は自分のしたいと思うとおりのことをし，他人がしていることに関心をもたない」は，「他人がしていることには何の関心も示さないで，自分のしたいことを，自分の責任で (on one's own) やろうと努める」と解するか，「人々は他人が何をしようと気にせず，自分の思うとおりにふるまう」(go one's own way) と訳す．「思われる」や「思うのだろう」などの日本語には，あまりとらわれる必要はない．

第7章　風俗・習慣

〈解　答　例〉

(i) Japanese people love following the fashion; probably they feel unhappy if they can't do the same thing as other people do. In Europe, however, people generally try to do what they want to do on their own, without showing any interest in what others are doing.

(ii) The Japanese people have a passion for following the fashion; they tend to be unhappy if they fail to do something similar to what others are doing. In West European countries, however, people generally don't care about what others do, but try to go their own way.

☆

〈例題 2〉

　欧米の国々では，誕生日やクリスマスやその他の特別な機会に，贈り物をするのが習わしである．しかし，贈り物をするのは，義務感からでなく，友情の気持ちでするのである．

■[語句]「その他の特別な機会に」on other special occasions /「義務感」a sense of duty, a sense of obligation

■[考え方]「贈り物をするのが習わしである」は，形式主語 it を用い，「贈り物を与える」の部分を不定詞句にする．つまり，It is customary to give presents. とする．「贈り物をするのは，義務感からでなく，友情の気持ちでするのです」は，「贈り物をするのは」は，動名詞構文を用い，主語とする．「義務感からでなく，友情の気持ちでする」は，not . . . , but ～ の相関接続詞を用いる．「友情の気持ちでする」を文脈から，「贈り物をするのは，すばらしいことだからだ」くらいに意訳する．

〈解　答　例〉

(i) In Europe and America people give presents to

one another on their birthdays, at Christmas time and on other special occasions. Giving presents, however, is not done out of a sense of duty, but simply because it is a nice thing to do.

(ii) In Europe and America it is customary to give gifts on birthdays, at Christmas and on certain other occasions. This is done, however, in a spirit of friendship rather than out of a sense of obligation.

☆

―――〈例題 3〉―――
この小さい町には，人なつっこさが充満している．テーブルマナーだの，エチケットだのというのは，西洋のどこかにたぶんあるのだろうけれど，ここではちょっとお目にかかれない．

■[語 句] 「人なつっこさ」⇨「好意的な雰囲気」an amiable atmosphere /「エチケット」etiquette

■[考え方] 「この小さい町には，人なつっこさが充満している」は，「ここは大変友情ある，小さな町である」と訳すか，「好意的な雰囲気がこの町に広まっている」と考え，A friendly atmosphere pervades [spreads through] this little town. とする．「テーブルマナーだの，エチケットだのというのは」は，「いわゆるテーブルマナーとかエチケットは」とするか，「われわれが知っているテーブルマナーやエチケットは」と解し，主語とする．この場合，table manners は複数扱い，etiquette は単数にすることに注意．「西洋のどこかに...あるのだろうけれど」は，「西洋のどこか他の地方に存在する (exist) だろうが」とするか，「西洋のどこか他の所に見い出されるだろうけれども」と解し，though probably found elsewhere in Europe とする．

〈解　答　例〉

(i)　This is a very friendly little town. Table manners and etiquette as we know them, probably exist in some other parts of the West, but they are not easily found around here.

(ii)　An amiable atmosphere pervades this little town. Here in this town what we call etiquette or good table manners, though probably found elsewhere in Europe, are not easily come across.

☆

――〈例題 4〉――

　食事のマナーについての日米の大きな違いは，日本では，食事中に話をするのはあまりよい作法とは思われないのに対し，アメリカでは，おいしい料理と同様，あるいはそれ以上にその場の会話が重要なウェートを占めていることだ．

■[語　句]　「食事のマナー」table manners /「日米の大きな違い」a great difference between Japan and America /「食事中」at (the) table

■[考え方]　「食事のマナーについての日米の大きな違いは」の部分を，「日米の間には，食事のマナーに大きな違いがある」とするか，日本文通り，「日米の大きな違いは」を主語にし，「日本では」で始まる部分を，that 節からなる補語とする．「食事中に話をするのは…よい作法とは思われない」は，it is … to ~ の文型を用い，it is not considered to be good manners to talk at the table とする．「アメリカでは，おいしい料理と同様，…それ以上にその場の会話が重要なウェートを占める」は，「食事中に話すことは」を補い，主語にし，「会話が料理と同様，いやそれ以上に重要である」と訳す．「おいしい料理」や

「その場の会話」の,「おいしい」とか「その場の」は訳出する必要はない.

〈解　答　例〉

(i) There is a great difference in table manners between Japan and America. In Japan it is not considered to be good manners to talk when you are eating, while in America conversation at the table is regarded as important as, or more important than, the food itself.

(ii) The big difference in table manners between Japan and the U.S. is that it is not regarded as very polite to chat at the table in Japan, but in America talking informally while eating is thought as much of (as), if not more of than, the food.

☆

┌─〈例題 5〉─────────────────┐
│　昔は, 家庭内での夫と妻の役割がはっきり区別されてい│
│た. 夫は会社や工場で働いて金をもうけ, 妻は家にいて子│
│供の世話や料理, 洗濯, 掃除などの家事をするのが当然と│
│考えられていた.│
└──────────────────────────┘

■[語 句]　「昔は」in the past, in former times /「夫と妻の役割」the roles of the husband and the wife /「金をもうける」earn money /「子供の世話をする」take care of children /「家事をする」do the housework /「当然と考えられる」be taken for granted, be considered natural

■[考え方]　「はっきり区別されていた」は,「夫の役割と妻の役割は, 非常に異なっていた」と解する.「...が当然と考えられていた」は, It was taken for granted that...が最も普通に用いられる構文.

〈 解　答　例 〉

(**i**)　In the past, the roles of the husband and the wife in the home were clearly defined. It was taken for granted that the husband worked in a company or a factory to earn money, while the wife stayed home, taking care of the children, and doing housework like cooking, washing and cleaning.

(**ii**)　In former times, the function of the husband was very different from that of the wife in the home. It was considered that the husband earned a living, working in an office or a factory, while the wife stayed home, looking after the children and doing domestic chores such as cooking, washing and cleaning.

第8章
趣味・娯楽・運動

Check & Check

〈趣味・娯楽〉

□~に趣味[興味]をもつ ⇨ be interested in, take [have, show] an interest in ~
　▶「弟は昆虫採集に興味をもっている」⇨ My brother has an interest in collecting insects.
　▶「切手収集の趣味があるかい」⇨ Do you go in for stamp collecting [collecting stamps]? go in for は take an interest in と同義

□あなたは何か楽器がひけますか ⇨ Can you play any (musical) instruments?

□私の趣味はギターを弾くことです ⇨ My hobby is playing the guitar.

第8章 趣味・娯楽・運動

▶hobby は,「余暇にする,切手収集や楽器をひくなどの静かな活動」. pastime や recreation なども同じように用いられ, pastime は「遊び」の意味に, recreation は「気分転換」の意をもつ

□うちの娘は服の趣味が良い ⇨ My daughter has good taste in clothes.
　▶この表現では taste は無冠詞. この taste は服飾のみならず, 家具, 言葉遣いなどの上品, 下品にも用いられる
　▶「私はアメリカ映画が好きです」⇨ I have a taste for American movies. cf. have a liking for ～ も同義の熟語

□彼はヘレンが自分の好みに合った ⇨ He found Helen perfectly to his taste.
　▶to his taste は to his liking と同義

□「映画と演劇ではどちらがお好きですか」「劇のほうです. 月に一度は芝居を見に行きます」⇨ "Which do you like better, movies or plays?" "I like plays better. I go to the theater once a month."
　▶「定期的に芝居見物をする人」を a theatergoer という

□フランス映画が, その映画館で上映中です ⇨ There is a French movie on at the cinema [theater].
　▶「上映中の」の意の on に注意

□チャップリン主演の映画 ⇨ a film starring Charlie Chaplin

□その映画で, ハムレットの役を演じたのはだれですか ⇨ Who played the part of Hamlet in that film?
　▶この play the part of を, 次の句と比較せよ. 「彼は政界で重要な役割を果たしている」⇨ He is playing an important part [role] in politics. この表現では, 不定冠詞と形容詞が用いられるのが普通

□その演劇は大当たりだ ⇨ The play was a box-office suc-

cess [hit].
　▶box office は「(劇場などの)切符売場」の意. box-office は,「大人気を呼ぶような」という意の形容詞

□学園祭で劇を上演する ⇨ give a play at the school festival

□入場料はいくらですか ⇨ What is the admission?
　▶「入場無料」《掲示》⇨ Admission free /「入場禁止」《掲示》⇨ No admittance. admittance は, 文字通り, ある場所に入ることについて, admission は, 比喩的に権利, 特権などを許されること

□映画を見に行く ⇨ go to the movies
　▶「いい映画を見る」⇨ see a good movie [film]

□そのストーリーを映画化する ⇨ make a movie of the story, make the story into a movie
　▶映画会社が「映画を作る」は, produce a film (of ～) という

□映画評 ⇨ a movie [film] review
　▶映画監督 ⇨ a film director / 映画俳優[女優] ⇨ a film actor [actress]

□記録映画 ⇨ a documentary film

□トランプをする ⇨ play cards
　▶この表現では, card は複数形で, 無冠詞

□トランプで運を占う ⇨ tell one's fortune from cards

□趣味と実益に ⇨ for profit and pleasure

□趣味で金もうけができればいいが ⇨ It would be very nice if I could make money out of my hobby.

□徹夜マージャンをする ⇨ stay up all night playing mah-jong [mah-jongg]

▶この stay up... ~ing は S+V+C の文型で，~ing が C (補語) となる分詞

□カナダ人の先生から英会話を習う ⇨ take lessons in English (conversation) from a Canadian teacher
　▶「ピアノを教える」⇨ give piano lessons. この場合，lesson はよく複数形になる

□写真を撮る ⇨ take a photograph [picture]
　▶「この写真を現像[焼きつけ]する」⇨ develop [print] this photo(graph) /「この写真を引き伸ばしてもらう」⇨ have this photo(graph) enlarged

□子供は写真の映りがいつもいい ⇨ Children always come out well in their photographs.

□アンは絵を描くのが好きです ⇨ Ann likes to draw pictures.
　▶draw は，ペンや鉛筆でかくこと，「絵の具を使って描く」は paint pictures とする

□絵の才能がある ⇨ have a talent [gift] for painting

□日曜画家 ⇨ a Sunday painter
　▶「日曜大工」の Sunday carpenter は和製英語. cf. a do-it-yourselfer

□合唱する ⇨ sing in chorus
　▶「ピアノの伴奏で歌う」⇨ sing to the piano /「斉唱(せいしょう)で歌う」⇨ sing in unison

□私は音痴です ⇨ I have no ear for music.
　▶「彼女は音楽がよく分かる」⇨ She has a good ear for music.

□このごろの若い人たちはラップに夢中です ⇨ These days young people are crazy about rap music.

□水彩画 ⇨ a water-color painting

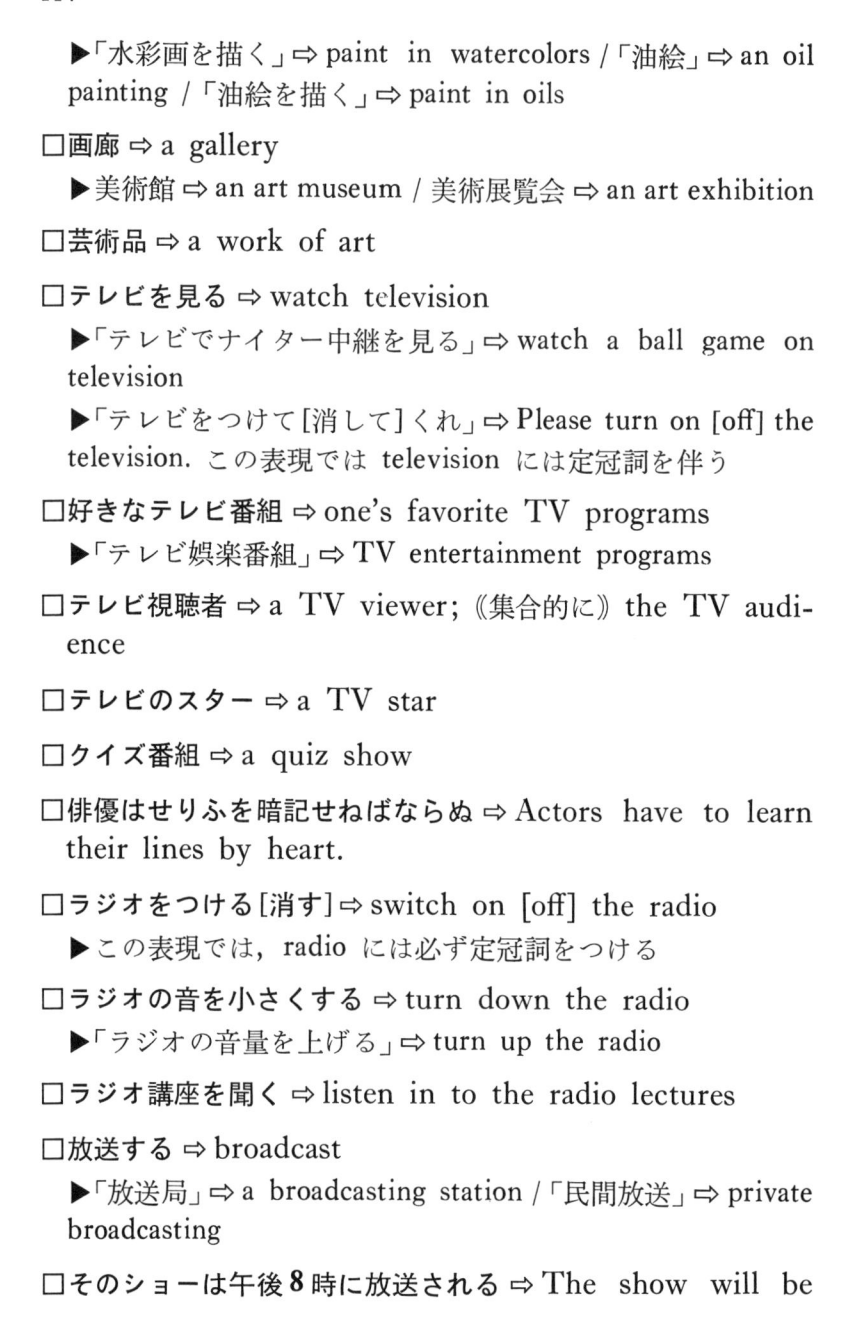

▶「水彩画を描く」⇨ paint in watercolors /「油絵」⇨ an oil painting /「油絵を描く」⇨ paint in oils

□画廊 ⇨ a gallery
　▶美術館 ⇨ an art museum / 美術展覧会 ⇨ an art exhibition
□芸術品 ⇨ a work of art
□テレビを見る ⇨ watch television
　▶「テレビでナイター中継を見る」⇨ watch a ball game on television
　▶「テレビをつけて[消して]くれ」⇨ Please turn on [off] the television. この表現では television には定冠詞を伴う
□好きなテレビ番組 ⇨ one's favorite TV programs
　▶「テレビ娯楽番組」⇨ TV entertainment programs
□テレビ視聴者 ⇨ a TV viewer;《集合的に》the TV audience
□テレビのスター ⇨ a TV star
□クイズ番組 ⇨ a quiz show
□俳優はせりふを暗記せねばならぬ ⇨ Actors have to learn their lines by heart.
□ラジオをつける[消す] ⇨ switch on [off] the radio
　▶この表現では，radio には必ず定冠詞をつける
□ラジオの音を小さくする ⇨ turn down the radio
　▶「ラジオの音量を上げる」⇨ turn up the radio
□ラジオ講座を聞く ⇨ listen in to the radio lectures
□放送する ⇨ broadcast
　▶「放送局」⇨ a broadcasting station /「民間放送」⇨ private broadcasting
□そのショーは午後8時に放送される ⇨ The show will be

on the air at 8 p.m.
  ▶「放送をやめる」は off the air という

□邦楽 ⇒ traditional Japanese music

□楽隊が美しい音楽を演奏した ⇒ The band played [performed] beautiful music.

□タコ揚げは昔，子供の好きな娯楽であった ⇒ Kite-flying used to be a favorite pastime for children.

□近くの川につりに行く ⇒ go fishing at [in, on] a nearby river
  ▶前置詞 at は魚つりをする地点を指し，in は魚つりをする地域一帯をいい，on はボートなどに乗って魚つりをすることをいう．go fishing to the river は誤り

□ハイキングに行く ⇒ go hiking, go on a hike

□スコットランドへ山登りに行く ⇒ go mountain-climbing in Scotland
  ▶go mountaineering は，山登りをプロにするときにいう
  ▶「山に行く」⇒ go to the mountains /「その山に登頂する」⇒ reach [climb to] the summit of the mountain

〈スポーツ・運動〉

□毎日運動しなさい ⇒ Get [Take] some exercise every day.
  ▶exercise は，「(身体を動かし体力をつける)運動」の意．exercise は，動詞としても用いられる

□大学でどんなスポーツをやりましたか ⇒ What sport(s) did you do [take part in] in college?
  ▶動詞の play は, tennis, baseball, football などの球技に使われる．「柔道をする」は practice judo という

□適度の運動 ⇒ moderate exercise
  ▶「運動不足のために」⇒ through lack of exercise

☐ボブスレー(そり競走)はアメリカで流行の冬のスポーツだ ⇨ Bobsleighing is a popular winter sport in America.

☐本校の運動会は10月5日に行なわれる ⇨ The athletic meet of our school will be held [take place] on October 5.
  ▶《英》では，通例 athletic meeting という

☐その野球の試合は雨天順延です ⇨ The baseball game will be postponed till the first fine day if it rains [in case of rain].

☐アテネ・オリンピック ⇨ the Athens Olympic Games
  ▶the Athens Olympics ともいう．「オリンピック開催都市」⇨ an Olympic city

☐国際競技 ⇨ an international athletic competition

☐2004年オリンピックの重量挙げの優勝者 ⇨ the 2004 Olympic victor in the weight-lifting competition

☐競技者 ⇨ a contestant
  ▶種目別の選手は, runner, swimmer, athlete, player...などとなる．「オリンピック出場選手」⇨ a member of the Olympic team

☐競技種目 ⇨ a sports event
  ▶「野外[屋内]競技」⇨ a field [an indoor] game

☐競技場 ⇨ a stadium
  ▶野球は a diamond, ゴルフは links, スケートは a rink, ボクシングは a ring などという

☐ゴルフは下手ですから，やり方を教えてください ⇨ Since I am poor at golf, please show me how to play it.

☐早大チームが優勝した ⇨ The Waseda University team

won the championship.

☐ 正々堂々とやる ⇨ play fair

☐ 試合に勝つ[負ける] ⇨ win [lose] a match
▶米国では, golf, cricket, tennis は match といい, baseball, football, basketball には game という. 剣道, 柔道, 相撲の試合は,「一勝負, 一番」を意味する bout をよく用い,「(勝ち抜きの)試合」は tournament という

☐ スキー・ジャンプで世界新記録をたてる ⇨ make a new world record in ski-jumping

☐ 観衆 ⇨ spectators

☐ 審判 ⇨ a referee, an umpire

☐ 国技 ⇨ the national sport

☐ 相撲を見に行く ⇨ go to see *sumo* wrestling matches

☐ テニスの決勝戦で勝つ[負ける] ⇨ win [lose] in the tennis finals
▶final は複数形で,「(競技などの)決勝戦」, または one's か, the を伴い「(学校の)期末試験」の意

☐ 彼女は美人コンテストで1等賞を取った ⇨ She won [took] first prize in the beauty contest.
▶この prize は通例, 無冠詞

☐ 100メートル競走でミッキーは1着になった ⇨ Mickey came in first place in the 100-meter dash.
▶came in の代わりに, got, took, won などが同義に用いられる. この「1位になる」の熟語では, place は無冠詞が通例

☐ そのチームを応援する ⇨ cheer the team

☐ 私たちは勝利チームのため万歳を三唱(さんしょう)した ⇨ We gave three cheers for the winning team.

Let's Try

【Ⅰ】 次の各英文が,それぞれ下の日本文に相当する意味になるように,(　)の中に適当な1語を入れなさい.
1. The girl has recently taken an (　　) in African music.
  (その娘は最近アフリカ音楽に関心をもってきた)
2. I have no (　　) for music.
  (私には音楽が全然わかりません)
3. It takes a lot of (　　) to be really good at tennis.
  (テニスに本当にうまくなるには十分な練習が必要です)
4. Who played the (　　) of Caesar?
  (だれがシーザーの役をやっていましたか)
5. Please dance (　　) your heart's content.
  (心ゆくまで踊ってください)

■[考え方] 頻出されるイディオムの知識を試す問題.
■[解答] 1. interest 2. ear 3. practice 4. part 5. to

【Ⅱ】 日本文の意味になるように,次の語を並べ換えなさい.
1. such as, places, on, publications, our school, and, athletics, emphasis, dramatics, activities, extracurricular
  (わが校は,演劇,出版,運動競技などの課外活動を重視しています)
2. winning, the Olympics, more, at, significant, participation, than, is
  (オリンピックは勝つことより参加することに意義がある)
3. He, race, meet, first, the 100-meter, at, the sports,

in, place, won
   (彼は運動会の100メートル競走で1等賞を取った)
4. Mt. Everest, showed, determination, to, to, firm, climb, he, the, summit, a, of
   (彼はエベレスト山頂まで登り切る堅い決意を示した)
5. genius, taste, pictures, rather, show, original, good, the, than
   (その絵は独創力は見られないが, 趣味のよさは現われている)

■[考え方] 1.「重視する」は place emphasis on とする. 主語をどれにするか. 2.「オリンピックは」とあるが,「オリンピックにおいては」と解する. 3.「1等賞を取った」は「1位を得た」とし, 無冠詞.「運動会」と「100メートル競走」の語順と前置詞に注意. 4.「堅い決意を示した」はSVOの文型で.「頂上まで」の前置詞に注意. 5.「独創力」は original genius. 全文を,「その絵は独創力よりも, 趣味のよさを示している」と解す

■[解答] 1. Our school places emphasis on extracurricular activities, such as dramatics, publications, and athletics. 2. At the Olympics, participation is more significant than winning. 3. He won first place in the 100-meter race at the sports meet. 4. He showed a firm determination to climb to the summit of Mt. Everest. 5. The pictures show good taste rather than original genius.

Let's Memorize

1. 適度な運動は健康に良い.
   A proper amount of exercise is good for your health.

2. 休み時間は外で運動するようにしよう.
   During the recess, let's try to get exercise outdoors.

3. 彼はスポーツは万能だが，特にテニスがうまい．

He is good at sports in general, but he is especially good at tennis.

4. 若者たちはスポーツに熱中することが多い．

Young people are often crazy about sports.

5. 私は体力をつけるために水泳を始めました．

I have started swimming to develop my physical strength.

6. 日本ではスポーツはなんでもやります．

We enjoy all kinds of sports in Japan.

7. 近ごろは，子どもが自由に遊べる場所が少なくなった．

Nowadays there are fewer and fewer places where children can play freely.

8. 父はいつも休日にゴルフに出かける．

My father usually goes to play golf on his days off.

9. 私は道楽に絵をはじめようと思っている．

I am thinking of taking up painting.

10. その映画に強烈な印象を受けた．

The film made a strong impression on me.

11. 彼女がその映画で主役を演じるだろう．

She will play the leading role in the movie.

12. ロックは特に若者に人気がある．

Rock music appeals especially to young people.

13. 弟は大のジャズ・ファンです．

My brother is a great jazz fan.

14. 叔父は，定年後，庭いじりに楽しみを見いだしている．

My uncle has found pleasure in gardening since retirement.

15. 彼女は趣味が広いので、話題に困らない。

She has a wide range of interests and is never at a loss for topics of conversation.

Exercises

―〈例題 1〉―
　私の父は教員で経済的には豊かとはいえなかったけれど，毎日の暮らしの中で楽しみを見つけることが上手な人でした．私がいろいろなものに興味を持って勉強するようになったのは，父の影響だと思います．

■[語句]「楽しみを見つける」find interest [pleasure] in /「～に興味を持つ」take an interest in ～

■[考え方]「経済的には豊かとはいえない」は，he was not rich か，he was not well [comfortably] off でよい．「経済的には」を financially と表現する必要はない．「毎日の暮らしの中で楽しみを見つけることが上手な人でした」は「日常生活の最も平凡な物事に興味を見つけることができる知識欲の盛んな人だ」とし，he was an inquisitive person who... とする．または，「日々の生活の些細なことから，面白いものを発見する能力をもっていた (have a gift for ～ing)」と訳出する．第2文の「私がいろいろなものに興味を持って勉強するようになったのは，父の影響だ」は，「父が私に大きな影響を与えてくれたために，私は多くのものに興味をもち，それらを勉強した」と考える．または，強調構文の it ～ that... を用いて，表現するのも良いだろう

〈解　答　例〉

(i) My father was a teacher and so we were not very rich, but he was an inquisitive person who found interest in the most ordinary things in daily life. It seems to me that, because of the great influence he had on me, I was able to take an interest in many things and study them.

(ii) Although my father was a teacher and I cannot possibly say that he was well off, he had a gift for finding something interesting in the little things of everyday life. I think it was due to his influence that I became interested in many things and began studying them.

☆

──〈例題 2〉──
たいていの人にとって，道楽はその職業と無関係なのが普通である．そういうわけで，日曜日に，医者は絵を描き，弁護士はシロウト大工になり，技師はつりをしに行くのである．

■[語 句] 「道楽」hobbies /「無関係である」have nothing to do with, have no connection with /「シロウト大工」an amateur carpenter

■[考え方] 「たいていの人にとって，道楽は...」は，「たいていの人の道楽は」とする．「普通である」は，副詞で usually か generally で表わす．「そういうわけで...である」は，That is why..., または「したがって...ということがある」と解し, Consequently, it often happens that... とする．

〈解 答 例〉

(i) Most people's hobbies usually have nothing to do with their occupations. That is why on Sundays a doctor paints pictures, a lawyer becomes an amateur carpenter, and an engineer goes fishing.

(ii) Generally, hobbies have no connection with occupations. Consequently, it often happens on Sundays that a physician is engaged in painting, a lawyer in carpentry, and an engineer in fishing.

☆

──〈例題 3〉──
　趣味は人によって異なる．屋外の運動を楽しむ者があり，音楽を楽しむ者もあり，また読書を楽しむ者もある．趣味をいちいち数えあげたらきりがない．人によって性格が異なる以上，これは当たり前のことである．だから他人の趣味をとやかく言うのは意味がない．

■[語句]　「屋外の運動」outdoor sports /「とやかく言う」criticize, find fault with /「～は意味がない」there is no point [sense] in ～ing, it is meaningless to ～ 不定詞

■[考え方]　「趣味は人によって異なる」は，Tastes differ [vary] from person to person. とするか，「人が異なれば，異なる趣味をもつ」とする．第2文の，「屋外の運動を楽しむ者があり，音楽を...あり，また読書を...もある」は，some people enjoy..., some music and others reading. とするか，Outdoor sports appeal to some people, music appeals to some and reading to others. と訳出できる．「趣味をいちいち数えあげたらきりがない」は，「趣味はあまりに多く，数えきれない」と考え，There are too many tastes to count. か，Tastes are too numerous to be counted. など，too...to ～ の相関語句を用いる．「人によって性格が異なる」は，「人が異なれば，異なる性格がある」とする．すなわち，Different people have different characters [personalities]. とすればよい

〈 解　答　例 〉
(i) Tastes differ from person to person. Some peo-

ple enjoy outdoor sports, some enjoy music, and others reading; there are too many tastes to count. This is natural enough, because different people have different characters. It is meaningless, therefore, to criticize other people's tastes.

(ii) Different people have different tastes. Outdoor sports appeal to some people, music appeals to some, and reading to others. Tastes are too numerous to be counted. This is taken for granted, because different people have different personalities. Therefore, there is no point in finding fault with other people's tastes.

☆

┌──〈例題 4〉──
│ テレビはわれわれを現実の世界から遠ざける．休みの日
│ など，天気が良くても部屋に閉じこもり，テレビのおもり
│ をしがちである．テレビは，マスコミのすぐれた媒体であ
│ るかもしれないが，われわれお互いの意志の疎通をさまた
│ げることが多い．

■[語 句]「現実の世界」the actual world, reality /「マスコミの媒体」a means of mass communication /「意志の疎通」communicate with other people, direct communication between people

■[考え方]「テレビはわれわれを現実の世界から遠ざける」は，「テレビは，現実の世界から離れた，新しい世界をわれわれに創造する」と解して，Television creates a new world for us, apart from the actual world. または，「テレビは，われわれを現実から切り離す」と考え，Television takes us away from reality. とする．「部屋に閉じこもり，テレビのおもり」は，「家にいて，テレビを見る」と簡単に訳す．「お互いの意志の疎通を

さまたげる」は「テレビは他人との意志の伝達をさまたげる」とか,「テレビは他人と意志を通じさせることをさまたげる」などと解する

〈 解　答　例 〉

(i)　Television creates a new world for us, apart from the actual world.　On holidays, you tend to stay home and watch television, even when the weather is nice.　It is true that television is an excellent means of mass communication, but it often interferes with direct communication between people.

(ii)　Television takes us away from reality.　On your days off, even when the weather is good, you feel like staying home to watch TV.　Television is certainly a great medium of mass communication, but it often keeps us from communicating with other people.

☆

──〈例題 5〉──
　　私は若いころ，いろいろ運動をやったが，何ひとつうまくならなかった．そこでだんだんやめていって，最後に残ったのが歩くことだけである．

■[語 句]　「運動をやる」take part in [go in for] sports /「～にうまくなる」be good at ～, become proficient in ～ /「やめる」give up, quit
■[考え方]　「何ひとつうまくならなかった」は,「どの運動にも，うまくならない」と解し，I failed to be good at any of them. または, I didn't become proficient in any of them. とする.「だんだんやめていった」は,「つぎつぎに，運動をやめた」と考え, gave them up one after another とする. one after another は，3つ以上のものにいい, one after the other

は，2つのものについていうのが通例.「最後に残ったのが...」は，前文から続けて so now... とか, until finally... とする. そのあとに,「運動のために私が今していることは，歩くことである」とか,「歩くことが, 私が今やっている唯一の運動である」と訳す.

<h+++>〈 解 答 例 〉</h+++>

(i) When I was young, I took part in various sports, but failed to be good at any of them. Then I gave them up one after another, so now the only thing I'm doing for exercise is walking.

(ii) In my youth I went in for a variety of sports, but I became proficient in none of them. So I quit them one after another, until finally I find walking is the only exercise I'm now getting.

第 9 章
天災・災難・事故

Check & Check

- □天災 ⇨ natural disasters
- □大惨事を招く ⇨ cause a serious disaster
- □災害地 ⇨ disaster areas
- □(火事や洪水の)罹災(りさい)者 ⇨ sufferers (from the fire or the flood)
  - ▶戦災者 ⇨ war sufferers / 地震の罹災者 ⇨ earthquake victims
- □昨夜の交通事故で 5 人の犠牲者が出た ⇨ Last night's traffic accident claimed [took] the lives of five people.
- □その鉄道事故で 10 名重傷者が出た ⇨ Ten people were seriously injured [hurt] in the railway accident.

▶同義表現：There were ten serious casualties in the train crash.

☐私は学校からの帰り道で事故にあった ⇨ I had an accident on my way home from school.
　▶「事故にあう」は meet with an accident ともいう

☐その交通事故は昨日ここで起きたのです ⇨ The traffic accident happened [occurred] here yesterday.
　▶here yesterday のように副詞の語順は「場所＋時間」が普通

☐幸いに彼は危うく一命をとりとめた ⇨ Fortunately he had a narrow escape from death.
　▶have a narrow escape は「危うく難を逃れる」の意の熟語．
　▶動詞表現：Fortunately he narrowly escaped being killed.

☐昨夜，地震のため，東海道新幹線のダイヤが乱れた ⇨ Because of last night's earthquake, the train schedules on the Tokaido Shinkansen were disrupted.

☐昨日の台風のため，鉄道が3時間不通になった ⇨ Because of the typhoon yesterday, the railway service was suspended [interrupted] for three hours.
　▶「不通になる」と「ダイヤが乱れる」の英文は，それぞれ主語が異なることに注意

☐地下鉄が停電のため，10分間止まった ⇨ The subway train stopped running [operating] for ten minutes because of a power failure.

☐彼の車が踏切で列車と衝突した ⇨ His car collided with a train at the railway crossing.

☐そのトラックが列車と衝突し，大破した ⇨ The truck came into collision with the train and was badly damaged.

第9章 天災・災難・事故

▶動詞の damage は無生物が主語になる

□この村は先週の洪水で大損害を受けた ⇨ This village suffered serious damage from the flood last week.
　▶動詞表現：This village was seriously damaged by the flood last week.

□その列車が脱線, 転覆した ⇨ The train was derailed and overturned.

□その台風は今年の稲作に大被害を与えた ⇨ The typhoon caused [did] heavy damage to the rice crops.
　▶名詞 damage は「損害」の意では, 不可算名詞.
　▶動詞表現：The typhoon heavily damaged the rice crops.

□九州南端に接近する台風 ⇨ a typhoon approaching the southern tip of Kyushu
　▶この approach は, 他動詞で, to を伴わない

□地震を予知する ⇨ predict an earthquake

□昨夜, 東京で大きい地震があった ⇨ We had a big earthquake in Tokyo last night.
　▶「地震」を主語にすると, A big earthquake hit [struck, shook] Tokyo last night. となる

□「今朝, 地震があったのを知っているかい」「いや, 知らなかった」⇨ "Did you feel the earthquake this morning?" "No, I didn't."

□日本は地震が多い ⇨ Earthquakes are frequent in Japan.

□この建物は地震に弱い ⇨ This building can't withstand an earthquake.
　▶「この建物は関東大震災の5倍の強さの地震に耐えられる」⇨ This building can withstand an earthquake five times as

strong as [stronger than] the Great Kanto Earthquake of 1923.

□東海道新幹線は雪に弱い ⇨ The Tokaido Shinkansen trains are easily affected by snowfalls.

□活[休, 死]火山 ⇨ an active [a dormant, an extinct] volcano
　▶「その山は火山活動をしている」⇨ The mountain is volcanically active.

□有珠山の噴火 ⇨ the eruption of Mt. Usu
　▶「噴火する」⇨ burst into eruption, erupt

□昨夜, 近所で火事が起きた ⇨ A fire broke out [started, occurred] in our neighborhood last night.
　▶break out は戦争や疫病の発生にも用いられる

□その火事の原因は漏電とされている ⇨ The fire is attributed to an electrical fault.

□その火事は1時間ばかりで消し止められた ⇨ The fire was put out [extinguished] in about an hour.

□彼の家が昨夜の火事で焼失した ⇨ His house burned down last night in the fire.
　▶この burned down の部分は, 受動態にして was burnt down とすることもできる

□2人の子供が昨夜の火事で焼死した ⇨ Two children were burnt to death in last night's fire.
　▶「凍死する」⇨ be frozen to death /「餓死する」⇨ be starved to death. この to は結果を示す

□消火器 ⇨ a fire extinguisher
　▶「火災報知器」⇨ a fire alarm [signal]

第9章 天災・災難・事故

- □非常出口 ⇨ an emergency exit [door]
- □救急車 ⇨ an ambulance
  - ▶「消防車」⇨ a fire engine [truck] /「救急所」⇨ a first-aid station
- □そのビルがガス爆発で破壊された ⇨ The building was wrecked [destroyed] by a gas explosion.
  - ▶「炭鉱の爆発」⇨ explosion in coal mines. この explosion は,「人口などの急激な増加」などにも用いられ, the population explosion という
- □洪水地 ⇨ a flooded area
- □その川が村一面に氾濫(はんらん)した ⇨ The river flooded the whole village.
  - ▶「豪雨で彼の家が浸水した」⇨ His house was flooded by the heavy rain.
- □豪雨が, この地方で洪水を引き起こしている ⇨ Heavy rains are causing floods in this part of the country.
  - ▶「豪雨のときは, よく大水になった」⇨ We often had floods when it rained hard.
- □九州南岸に津波がおそった ⇨ A tidal wave swept [struck] the south coast of Kyushu.
- □天災は忘れたころに起こる ⇨ Natural disasters strike (us) when we least expect them.
  - ▶「忘れたころ」は,「予期しないとき」と考える
- □雷が私の家の近くの木に落ちた ⇨ Lightning struck [hit] a tree near my house.
  - ▶「落ちた」を fell on とするのは誤り. ここでは,「雷鳴」の意の thunder は用いられない
- □今日でも, アフリカでは飢饉(きん)で苦しんでいる人々がたく

さんいる ⇨ Even today many people in Africa are suffering because of famine.

□車の事故で, 3人が軽[重]傷を負った ⇨ Three people were slightly [seriously] injured in the car accident.

▶人を主語にし,「負傷」を表わす文では, 受動態を用いる. 負傷者の人数が確認されないときは,「数人が死亡したと報ぜられた」とし, A number of people were reported killed. となる. この report は, 目的補語を伴って「...だと報じる」の意

▶「交通事故」では, be injured, be hurt で「負傷する」の意を表わす. be wounded は, 戦争などでの負傷に用いる

▶injure の名詞形は, injury. injury を用いて, 上の和文を英訳すると, Three people got [received] serious injuries in the car accident. となる

□高速度で走行中に, 車のタイヤがパンクしたら, 恐ろしい事故が起こるだろう ⇨ If you have a blowout while driving at (a) high speed, there will probably be a terrible accident.

▶「パンクする」は, 主語が「人・車」のとき, have a blowout [a puncture] (動作), have a flat tire (状態);「タイヤ」のときは, blow out, get punctured という

□車の台数が増加すれば, 事故もそれだけ多くなるだろう ⇨ The more cars there are, the more accidents there will be.

□彼は飲酒運転で罰金を科せられた ⇨ He was fined for drunk(en) driving.

▶drunk(en) driving は, driving while (he was) drunk としてもよい. drunken は, 名詞の前で形容詞的に(限定用法), drunk は, 常に叙述的に用いられる (例えば, He is *drunk*. という形). しかし, 今日では drunken の代わりに, drunk が

第9章　天災・災難・事故

使われることも多い

☐ 環境汚染は日本ばかりでなく，世界全般が直面している最も深刻な社会問題の一つである ⇨ Environmental pollution is one of the most serious social problems that confront not only Japan, but also the rest of the world.
▶「その地域の人々は大気汚染に苦しんでいる」⇨ The people in that area are troubled by air pollution. /「騒音公害」⇨ noise pollution

☐ 放射能で汚染された空気 ⇨ air polluted [contaminated] by radioactivity

☐ 工場廃液による河川の汚染 ⇨ industrial pollution of a river

☐ そのジェット機は緊急着陸したが，幸い死傷者はなかった ⇨ The jet plane made an emergency landing, but fortunately there were no casualties.

Let's Try

【Ⅰ】下の囲みに与えられている動詞を，英文の空所に入れ，（　）内の日本文の意味になるよう完成しなさい．

1. Something (　　) wrong with the train and it stopped for ten minutes.
   (電車が故障して，10分間止まった)
2. My car (　　) down on the way to the airport, and I had to get a taxi.
   (空港に行く途中，車が故障し，タクシーをひろわねばならなかった)
3. The old house (　　) down and only ashes were left.
   (古い家が焼けおち，灰になった)

天災・災難・事故

4. On our trip to Kyushu, one of our tires (　　) out.

(九州へ旅行中に，タイヤがパンクした)

5. Why doesn't he drive more carefully? He almost (　　) over that child.

(どうしてもっと注意して運転しないのか．あの子供をひきそうになったのに)

6. The fire fighters worked hard, but were not able to (　　) out the fire.

(消防士たちが懸命にやったが，消火できなかった)

ran　　blew　　went　　broke　　put　　burned

■[ヒント] 1.「故障している」(状態) は Something is wrong with the train. という．動作は？ 2. 車などの機械が故障する (=stop working) は？ 3.「焼失する」 4. タイヤが主語のときは，got punctured ともいう． 5.「ひく」 6. =extinguish

■[解答] 1. went　2. broke　3. burned　4. blew　5. ran　6. put

[II] 日本文の意味に合うように（　　）内の語句を並べ換えなさい．

1. 昨夜だれかに自転車を盗まれた．
(my bicycle, had, last night, I, stolen)

2. 天災は避けがたいものだ．
(escape, it, natural disasters, to, hard, is)

3. 不幸にも彼の乗った飛行機が墜落した．
(he was, it was, the plane, crashed, unfortunate that, in)

4. 昨夜の地震のため，この地方に住む多くの人々が家を失った．

第9章　天災・災難・事故

(many people, homeless, earthquake, living, last night's, here, left)
5.　台風のために列車の到着が遅れている．
(train arrivals, schedule, to, behind, the typhoon, are, due)
6.　水質汚染で川から魚の姿が消えてしまった．
(water pollution, fish, the river, of, from, because, have, disappeared)

■[ヒント]　1. have＋目的語＋過去分詞の文型．　2. 形式主語に it を用い，to 不定詞を真主語に．　3.「彼の乗った」を he was in とする．　4. S＋V＋O＋C の文型．　5.「遅れる」は behind time ともいう．　6.「水質汚染で」は「水質汚染のため」と解す

■[解答]　1. I had my bicycle stolen last night.　2. It is hard to escape natural disasters.　3. It was unfortunate that the plane he was in crashed.　4. Last night's earthquake left many people living here homeless.　5. Due to the typhoon, train arrivals are behind schedule. (due to the typhoon を文尾に置いてもよい)　6. Fish have disappeared from the river because of water pollution. (Because of water pollution を文頭にしてもよい)

Let's Memorize

1.　その事故を考えただけで，私はぞっとする．
The mere thought of the accident made me shudder.

2.　大地震がこの地方に起こるといううわさがある．
Rumor has it that a big earthquake will occur in this area.

3.　今朝の地震で，列車のダ
The trains aren't running

イヤが乱れている. | on schedule because of the earthquake this morning.

4. その列車の脱線事故で, たくさんの怪我人が出た. | The train derailment left many people injured.

5. 警察は列車事故の原因を目下, 調査している. | The police are now investigating the cause of the train accident.

6. 火事で家を焼失し, 彼は途方にくれてしまった. | He was at a loss what to do when his house burned down.

7. 私が泊まっていたホテルが火事になったが, 幸運に死なずにすんだ. | A fire broke out at the hotel where I was staying, but fortunately I escaped death.

8. 大雨のあとの山崩れで, 家がたくさんつぶれた. | Many houses were destroyed by the landslides after the heavy rain.

9. 昨夜の大雨で, 町に水が出た. | Last night's heavy rain flooded the town.

10. この通り沿いの住人は騒音公害に悩まされている. | The people living along this street are troubled by noise pollution.

11. その飛行機事故で, 多くの乗客が死傷した. | Many passengers were killed or injured in the plane crash.

12. その飛行機墜落は人災だと, 考えているものが多い. | Many people believe that the plane crash was caused by human error.

13. 彼は酔っ払い運転で事故 | He caused a car accident

第9章　天災・災難・事故

を起こした.	because of drunk(en) driving.
14. その川は汚染がひどく，魚がもう住んでいない.	The river is so polluted that fish can no longer live in it.
15. ガス爆発の現場は，目もあてられないひどさだ.	The scene of the gas explosion was too horrible to look at.

Exercises

〈例題 1〉

> マグニチュード 6.6 の強い地震が，昨日午前 11 時，北海道から中国地方に至る日本の広い地域を襲い，2 名が死亡，56 名が重傷，列車が停止，多くのビルの窓ガラスがひどく破損したと，今日の新聞が報じている.

■[語句]「マグニチュード 6.6」measuring [registering] 6.6 on the Richter scale /「襲う」hit, strike

■[考え方]　全文を 2 つの部分に分ける．つまり，「強い地震が...日本の広い地域を襲った」と，「2 名が死亡，56 名が重傷...窓ガラスがひどく破損した」の 2 つの部分に．前半は，Today's newspaper says に，後半は According to the report, に続ける．「死亡」や「負傷」は，他動詞の kill, injure を用い，受動態で表現する

〈解　答　例〉

(i) Today's newspaper says that a strong earthquake measuring 6.6 on the Richter scale hit many parts of Japan from Hokkaido to Chugoku at 11 o'clock yesterday morning. According to the report, two people were killed and fifty-six seriously injured. Trains stopped running, and the windowpanes in many buildings were badly damaged.

(ii) According to today's newspaper, a sharp earthquake registering 6.6 on the Richter scale struck a wide area of Japan from Hokkaido to the Chugoku region at eleven a.m. yesterday, killing 2 people and seriously wounding 56 others. Trains were brought to a stop, and the windowpanes of many buildings were shattered.

☆

――〈例題 2〉――
　ナマズがなんの訳もなく興奮し，泳ぎ出すと，強い地震が起こるということが，昔から日本で言われてきた．今日，科学者たちは，これを研究し，両者に関係があるか否か発見しようとしている．

■[語句]　「ナマズ」a catfish /「なんの訳もなく」for no particular [apparent] reason

■[考え方]　第1文は，「ナマズが...泳ぎ出すと，強い地震が起こる」を名詞節にする．「昔から日本で言われてきた」は，It has long been said in Japan that... とするか，「昔，日本では，人々が...に気がついていた」と解し，In ancient times in Japan, people noticed that... と訳す．「ナマズが...泳ぎ出すと，強い地震が起こる」の名詞節における時制は，(i) 現在時制，(ii) 過去時制にする．「科学者たちは，これを研究し...発見しようとしている」は，「科学者たちは，両者に関係があるか否か発見するために，この考えを研究している」と解す

〈解　答　例〉

(i) It has long been said in Japan that if catfish become agitated and swim around in an excited manner, for no particular reason, a strong earthquake is likely to hit. Scientists are now studying this matter to find out whether there is a connection between the two.

(ii) In ancient times in Japan, people noticed that whenever catfish started swimming around wildly for no apparent reason, an earthquake would usually occur. Scientists today are working on this idea to see if there really is a relation between these.

☆

──〈例題 3〉──
　行楽客を満載した客船が，マニラの南176キロメートルのミンドロ島沖で，油運送船と衝突，炎上し，沈没，約1,500人が溺死した．これは今世紀最悪の海難事故であろう．

■[語 句]　「行楽客」a holiday-maker, a vacationist /「客船」a passenger ship [boat] /「油運送船」an oil tanker /「～と衝突」collide with ～, come into collision with ～ /「海難事故」a maritime disaster

■[考え方]　まず，「衝突」「炎上」「沈没」「溺死」の順序に英訳に取り組む．動詞を中心に言い換え，「行楽客で混んでいた客船が油運送船と衝突し，燃え上がり，沈没し，約1,500人が溺死した」とする．地点を示す「マニラの南176キロメートルのミンドロ島沖で」は，「衝突」の後に，または「沈没」の後に，off the coast of Mindoro Island, 176 kilometers south of Manila とすればよい

〈解　答　例〉

(i) A passenger ship crowded with holiday-makers collided with an oil tanker off the coast of Mindoro Island, 176 kilometers south of Manila. It started burning and sank, drowning nearly 1,500 people. This is probably one of the worst maritime disasters (of) this century.

(ii) Nearly 1,500 people were drowned after a passenger boat jammed with holiday travelers came into collision with an oil tanker, burst into flames and sank off the coast of Mindoro Island, 176 kilometers south of Manila. This may be one of the biggest disasters at sea the world has seen this century.

☆

┌─〈例題 4〉─────────────────┐
│ 昨夜，その台風は東海地方を襲い，米作に多大な被害を │
│ 及ぼし，何百という家々が浸水した．今朝もまだ，列車の │
│ ダイヤが乱れ，東京周辺の通勤者に不便を与えている． │
└────────────────────┘

■[語 句]　「東海地方」the Tokai area /「〜に多大な被害を及ぼす」do a lot of damage to 〜 /「東京周辺の」in and around Tokyo /「通勤者」commuters /「〜に不便を与える」cause inconvenience to 〜

■[考え方]　第1文は，「台風」を主語にすればよい．「何百という家々が浸水」は，「〜という家々が水中下に残された」と解し S+V+O+C の文型を用いる．「列車のダイヤが乱れ」は，「列車の時間表が乱れる」とか，「列車が予定通りに運行していない」と解する．「〜に不便を与えている」の部分に，結果を表わす to を用い，to the annoyance of commuters とすることもできる

〈解　答　例〉

(i) Last night the typhoon hit the Tokai area, did a lot of damage to the rice crops, and left hundreds of houses under water. This morning the railway schedules are still considerably disrupted, causing great inconvenience to commuters in and around Tokyo.

(ii) Due to the typhoon, which struck the Tokai area last night, the rice crop was seriously damaged and hundreds of houses flooded. This morning the trains in and around Tokyo are still not running on schedule, to the annoyance of the people going to work.

☆

―――〈例題 5〉―――
A:「困った顔しているじゃないか．どうしたんだい」
B:「昨日，駅の近くの路上にとめておいた自転車を盗まれてしまったんだ」
A:「警察にそんなことを届けても，そんな所にとめておくべきではなかったと注意されるのが関の山だろう」
B:「多分ね」

■[語 句]「困った顔」look upset, look depressed /「どうしたんだい」What's up?, What's wrong?
■[考え方]「路上にとめておいた自転車を盗まれた」は，have＋目的語＋過去分詞か受動態の構文，または someone を主語にし V＋目的語の 3 通りに訳せる．「警察にそんなことを届けても～と注意されるのが関の山だろう」は，「そのことについて警察に不平を言っても～と警告されるに過ぎない」くらいにする．「～のが関の山だろう」は，All they can do is (to) ～ の構文を用いる．「とめておくべきではなかった」は should not have left it とする．「多分ね」は，「おそらく，君の言う通りだろう」と訳す

〈解 答 例〉

(i) A: You look upset. What's up?
　　B: Yesterday the bicycle I left on the street near

the station was stolen.

A: If you complain to the police about it, all they will do is (to) tell you that you should not have left it there.

B: Probably you are right.

(ii) A: You look depressed. What's wrong?

B: Yesterday someone stole the bicycle I left on the street close to the railroad station.

A: Even if you go to the police to report (on) it, they will only warn you that you ought not to have left your bicycle at such a place.

B: I'm afraid so.

第10章
読書・語学

Check & Check

〈読　書〉
- 愛読書 ⇨ one's favorite book
- 傑作 ⇨ a masterpiece, a masterwork
- 読書好き ⇨ a book lover, a bookworm
- 多くの本を手当たり次第に読むより，少数の本を精読する方がよい ⇨ It is better to read a few books carefully than to read many at random.
- 速[多]読する ⇨ read rapidly [extensively]
- 深く読む ⇨ read deeply
  - ▶「言外の意味を読む」⇨ read between the lines
- とばし読みが下手です ⇨ I am not good at skimming

(books).
▶skim は read hastily「ざっと読む」の意

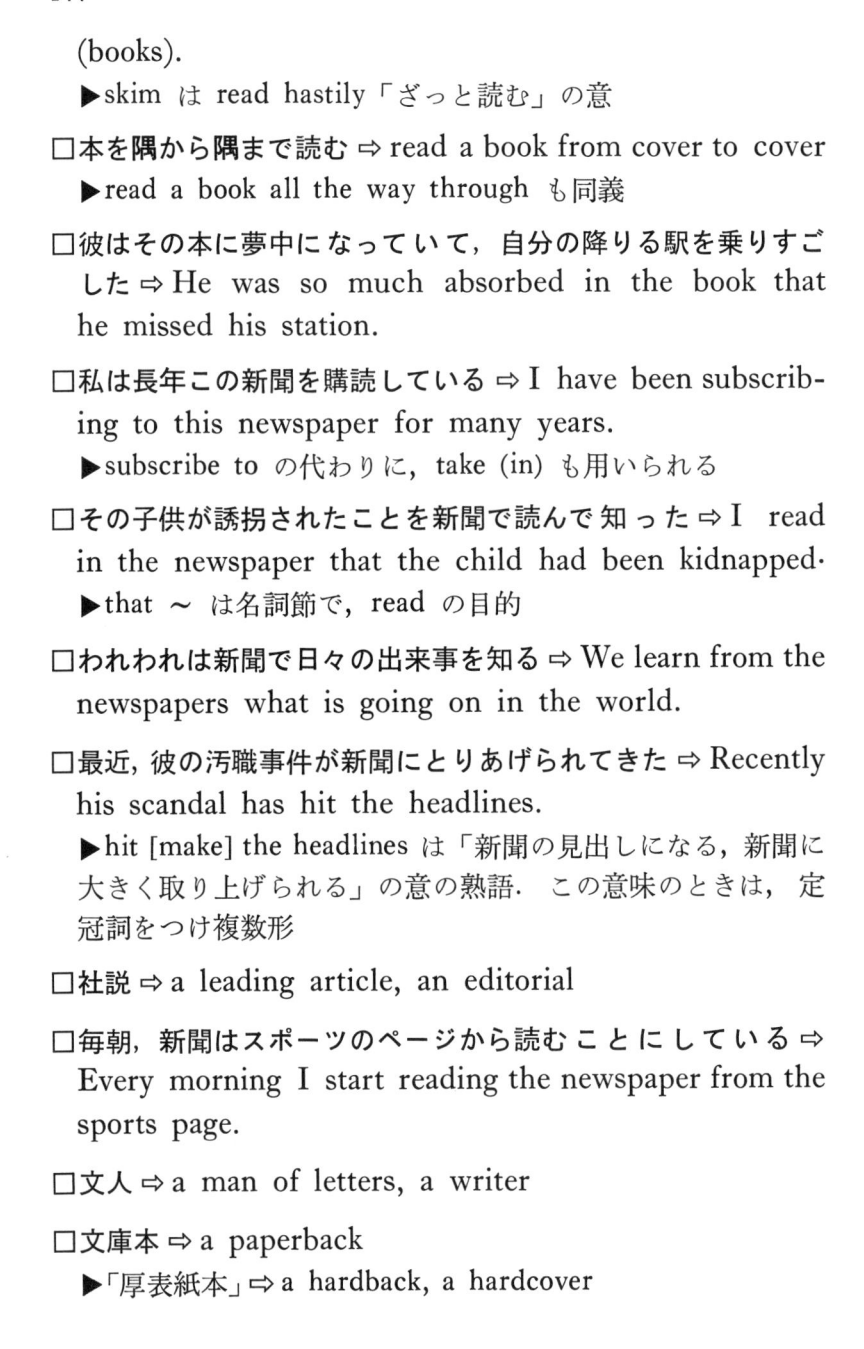

☐本を隅から隅まで読む ⇨ read a book from cover to cover
▶read a book all the way through も同義

☐彼はその本に夢中になっていて，自分の降りる駅を乗りすごした ⇨ He was so much absorbed in the book that he missed his station.

☐私は長年この新聞を購読している ⇨ I have been subscribing to this newspaper for many years.
▶subscribe to の代わりに，take (in) も用いられる

☐その子供が誘拐されたことを新聞で読んで知った ⇨ I read in the newspaper that the child had been kidnapped.
▶that ～ は名詞節で，read の目的

☐われわれは新聞で日々の出来事を知る ⇨ We learn from the newspapers what is going on in the world.

☐最近，彼の汚職事件が新聞にとりあげられてきた ⇨ Recently his scandal has hit the headlines.
▶hit [make] the headlines は「新聞の見出しになる，新聞に大きく取り上げられる」の意の熟語．この意味のときは，定冠詞をつけ複数形

☐社説 ⇨ a leading article, an editorial

☐毎朝，新聞はスポーツのページから読むことにしている ⇨ Every morning I start reading the newspaper from the sports page.

☐文人 ⇨ a man of letters, a writer

☐文庫本 ⇨ a paperback
▶「厚表紙本」⇨ a hardback, a hardcover

第10章 読書・語学

□彼の新しい本はいつ出版されるのですか ⇨ When will his new book come out?
　▶come out は be published と同義
□その本はまだ印刷になっていない ⇨ The book is not in print yet.
　▶「絶版である」⇨ out of print
□私は新刊書を数冊英国に注文した ⇨ I have ordered some new books from England.
　▶前置詞に注意．I have written to England for some new books. ともいう
□この新聞の1日の発行部数は100万部です ⇨ This newspaper has a daily circulation of one million.
　▶この circulation は不定冠詞 a を伴う．「その雑誌の発行部数は多い」⇨ The magazine has a wide [good] circulation.
□多数の中から一冊選ぶ ⇨ choose a book from among many
□近ごろ新刊書が多くて，選択に困る ⇨ There have been so many new books published recently that I am at a loss which to choose.
□忙しくて読書する時間がないとこぼす人が多い ⇨ Many people complain that they are too busy to find time for reading.
□昨夜はその小説を読んで夜ふかしした ⇨ I stayed up till late last night reading the novel.
□読書しながら眠る ⇨ doze over a book
□書物を古本で買う ⇨ buy a book secondhand
　▶この secondhand は副詞．「古本屋」⇨ a secondhand bookshop. この secondhand は形容詞

□トルストイの小説を翻訳で読む ⇨ read Tolstoi's novels in translation
□この小説はフランスの原書から翻訳したものだ ⇨ This novel is a translation from the French original.
□化学の良い参考書を推薦していただけますか ⇨ Can you recommend me a good reference book on chemistry?
　▶Can you recommend a good reference book on chemistry to me? ともいう
□漫画本 ⇨ a comic book
　▶「4コマの漫画」⇨ a (comic) strip

〈語　学〉
□子供は新しい言葉を聞き覚えるのが早い ⇨ Children are quick at picking up new words.
　▶pick up は「(偶然に)聞き覚える」の意
□英会話を習う ⇨ learn to speak English
　▶learn English conversation は, 和製英語表現で誤り. learn how to speak English もよい
□彼女は毎晩, 彼と電話で長話をする ⇨ She carries on [has] a long conversation with him over the telephone every night.
　▶この conversation には不定冠詞 a をつけて用いる
□私は高校時代, 英語の勉強で苦労した ⇨ When I was in high school, I had difficulty [trouble] (in) studying English.
　▶この構文では, have difficulty のあとに to 不定詞は用いられない
□英語を用いる諸国民 ⇨ English-speaking peoples
　▶英語を母国語とする人 ⇨ a native speaker of English

第10章　読書・語学

- □語学 ⇨ language study, linguistics
  - ▶「語学の教師」⇨ a language teacher /「語学者」⇨ a linguist /「語学が達者[弱い]」⇨ be a good [poor] linguist
- □語学の習得には，根気と勤勉さが必要だ ⇨ It takes patience and industry to learn a language.
- □口語で ⇨ in spoken [colloquial] language
- □君はいつ外国語を習い始めるつもりですか ⇨ When do you intend to take up a foreign language?
  - ▶「英語を習い始める」は，language に定冠詞をつけ，take up the English language という．しかし，language を除き take up English というのが普通
- □彼はいなか丸出しのなまりで話す ⇨ He speaks in a broad accent.
  - ▶broad は「お国なまり丸出しの」の意の形容詞
- □無口な[おしゃべりな]人 ⇨ a quiet [talkative] person
  - ▶「お茶を飲みながら雑談する」⇨ chat over a cup of tea
- □自由に英語を使いこなす ⇨ have a good command of English
  - ▶この command は「(言語などを)使いこなす力」の意．不定冠詞と形容詞をつけて用いる
- □そのスイスの娘は，3ヵ国語が流暢(りゅうちょう)だ ⇨ The Swiss girl is fluent in three languages.
- □1年や2年で，外国語に熟達するのはむずかしい ⇨ It is difficult to attain proficiency in a foreign language in a year or two.
  - ▶「〜に熟達する」は，become proficient in 〜 ともいう
- □英語で用をたすことができる ⇨ be able to say what one wants in English

▶「英語で自分の考えを人にわからせる」⇨ make oneself understood in English

□アメリカ人の先生から英語を習う ⇨ learn English from an American teacher
　▶この from の代わりに, under や with も用いられる

□私は英語を5年も勉強してきたが, まだ英語で満足に手紙も書けない ⇨ I have been studying English for five years, but I still haven't learned to write letters in English satisfactorily.
　▶study は,「勉強[研究]する」, learn to ～ は「身につける, できるようになる」の意

□人は経験で学ぶ ⇨ People learn from [by] experience.
　▶「模倣で学ぶ」⇨ learn by imitation /「その詩を暗記する」⇨ learn the poem by heart, memorize the poem

□彼は話題が豊富だ ⇨ He has a rich stock of topics.

□その風景の美しさは言葉では表わせないほどだ ⇨ The scenery is too beautiful for words.
　▶The beauty of the scenery is beyond description. も同義の表現

□失言する ⇨ make a slip of the tongue
　▶「書き誤り」を a slip of the pen という

□母国語としてフランス語を話す ⇨ speak French as one's mother tongue

□だまっている ⇨ hold one's tongue
　▶この熟語は remain silent と同義で, 通例, 命令する際に用いられる

□君の本心を恋人に打ち明けなさい ⇨ You should speak your mind to your girlfriend.

第10章 読書・語学

▶speak one's mind は「思っていることを率直に言う」の意

□彼は何か気にかかることがあるに違いない ⇨ He must have something on his mind.
　▶have ～ on one's mind は「～を心配している，～を気にかけている」の意

□自分の思っていることを，他人の感情を害さず，言うのはむずかしい ⇨ It is difficult to say what you are thinking without hurting other people's feelings.
　▶without hurting other people's feelings を，without offending other people としてもよい

□その問題について意見を言う ⇨ give [express] one's opinion on the subject
　▶「意見をいう」を *say* one's opinion とするのは誤り

□人に話しかける ⇨ speak [talk] to a person

□ビルの意見によると，英語は日本語より修得がむずかしいという ⇨ In Bill's opinion, English is more difficult to learn than Japanese.
　▶「ビルの意見によると」を according to Bill's opinion とするのは誤り．According to Bill が正用法．Bill is of the opinion that ～ ともいう

□彼は自分の考えを明瞭に英語で表現する能力がある ⇨ He has the ability to express himself in good clear English.
　▶express oneself は，「自分の考えや感情を言葉で書いたり，話して表現する」の意
　▶have the ability のあとは，to 不定詞を用いるのが普通

□英語にうまくなりたいなら，間違いを恐れてはならぬ ⇨ If you want to be good at English, you must not be afraid of making mistakes.

□彼は大学でドイツ語を専攻した ⇨ He majored in German in college.
□彼の言おうとしていることがわかりますか ⇨ Can you make out what he is trying to say?
　▶make out は, understand と同義
□外国に旅行中, 言葉が通じないと不自由である ⇨ When we are traveling abroad, it is inconvenient to be unable to make ourselves understood.
　▶(in)convenient は, it や無生物が主語となる
□父はパリに行くため, フランス語をやり直すつもりだ ⇨ My father is thinking of brushing up his French before going to France.
　▶brush up ～ は,「～の勉強をやり直す」の意
□ペルーでは何語を話していますか ⇨ What language do they speak in Peru?
　▶この they は people でもよい. What language is spoken in Peru? も同義
□英語は国際語で, 世界中で話されている ⇨ English is an international language, and is now spoken [used] all over the world.

Let's Try

【I】 次の英文が日本文の意味になるよう (　　　) 内に与えられている語のうち, 適当なものを選びなさい.

1. He has (learned, picked) up such excellent English just by living in America for some years.
　（彼はアメリカに数年住んだだけで, あんな立派な英語を聞き覚えた）

2. I was (absorbed, devoted) in a book and didn't hear you call.
   (本に熱中していたので、呼ぶ声が聞こえなかった)
3. Please let me (bring, have) the book I lent you the other day.
   (先日お貸しした本をお返しください)
4. In reading, you should read between the (meanings, lines).
   (本を読むときは、言外の意味を読み取るべきだ)
5. He has a good (ability, command) of English.
   (彼は英語を自由に使いこなす能力がある)
6. How do you (think about, feel about) this book?
   (この本をどうお考えですか)
7. It's become (usual, common) in Japan for even elementary school children to learn English.
   (小学生のあいだで英語を習うことが日本で盛んになっている)
8. I must (improve, brush) up my Italian before I go to Rome.
   (ローマに旅行する前に、イタリア語をやり直さねばならぬ)

■[ヒント] 1. どちらも「覚える」意. 2. devoted のあとは in でよいか. 3. Please bring me the book なら正しい. 4. 「行間から隠れている意味を発見する」の意. 5. He has the ability to speak English well. と同義にする. 6. How do you like this book? / What do you think about this book? は、いずれも正用法. feel about ～「～ついて感想を抱く」 7. 「盛んになる」は、「普及している」意. 8. 「やり直す」は「復習する」意
■[解答] 1. picked 2. absorbed 3. have 4. lines 5. command 6. feel about 7. common 8. brush

【II】 次の書き出しの英文につづけて，下の語句を適当に配列し，日本文の意味を表わしなさい．
1. No matter ＿＿＿＿＿＿＿＿＿＿＿＿＿＿＿＿＿．
 (I, halfway, dull, a book is, can't, how, it, down, put)
 どんなに退屈な本でも，私は途中で放り出すことができません．
2. That novel＿＿＿＿＿＿＿＿＿＿＿＿＿＿＿＿．
 (experience when, based, young, the writer's, is, he was, on)
 その小説は作者の若いときの経験をもとにしている．
3. My grandfather＿＿＿＿＿＿＿＿＿＿＿＿＿．
 (a newspaper, glasses, doesn't, read, need, to)
 祖父は眼鏡がなくても新聞が読める．
4. When I was ＿＿＿＿＿＿＿＿＿＿＿＿＿＿＿．
 (expressing, in English, in college, myself, difficulty, I had, in, a lot of)
 大学生のとき，私は英語で自分の思うことを表現することがとても困難であった．

■[ヒント] 1. No matter＋how＋形容詞＋S＋V の譲歩構文の語順に注意. 2.「もとにしている」は be based on と受動態にする. 3. 和文を直訳すると, My grandfather can read a newspaper without using glasses. となる. 4.「～が困難である」は have difficulty in ～ing の構文を用いる.

■[解答] 1. No matter how dull a book is, I can't put it down halfway. 2. That novel is based on the writer's experience when he was young. 3. My grandfather doesn't need glasses to read a newspaper. 4. When I was in college, I had a lot of difficulty in expressing myself in English.

Let's Memorize

1. 読書は私の大きな楽しみです。

    Reading is a great pleasure to me.

2. 私はかたい本よりも、やわらかい本を読むのが好きです。

    I prefer light reading to serious books.

3. そのアメリカ人の学者は、日本の古典文学研究に熱中している。

    The American scholar is absorbed in the study of Japanese classical literature.

4. 用済みになったら、本を元のところへ戻しなさい。

    Put the book where it was when you have done with it.

5. 彼の小説が文学界で大きな反響を起こした。

    His novel has caused a great sensation in the literary world.

6. 本を読むときは、ゆっくり、そして繰り返して読むべきです。

    When you read a book, you should read it slowly and repeatedly.

7. この探偵小説はとても良かったので一気に読んでしまった。

    This detective story was so good that I read it in one sitting.

8. この週刊誌は発行部数では日本一です。

    This weekly magazine has the largest circulation in Japan.

9. 単語の意味が分からないなら、辞書を引きなさい。

    If you don't understand the meaning of a word, look it up in the dictionary.

10. その娘は自分の英語力を

    The girl boasts about her

自慢している．

11. 英語では考えを満足に述べられないので，がっかりすることがある．

12. 昨年，アメリカに行ったとき，英語が分からなかったが，なんとか身振りで話をした．

13. 英語が流暢(りゅうちょう)に話せたら，どんなに素晴らしいだろう．

14. 学校の勉強だけでは，英会話の力はなかなかつかない．

15. この本はやさしい英語で書かれている．

ability to speak English.

I can't express myself satisfactorily in English and it's often disappointing.

When I was in America last year, I could hardly understand a word of English, but I managed to communicate with gestures.

How nice it would be to be able to speak English fluently!

You don't really get good at speaking English just by studying at school.

This book is written in easy English.

Exercises

――〈例題 1〉――
このごろの若い者はあまり本を読まないとなげく人がいるが，本を読む量が減ったからといって，若い人の知的欲求が少なくなったと即断しては間違いでしょう．

■[語句]「なげく」complain, express regret /「知的欲求」desire [thirst] for knowledge /「～と即断する」jump to the conclusion that ～, form the hasty conclusion that ～

■[考え方]「このごろの若い者」は，young people these days とする．「本を読む量が減ったからといって...知的欲求が少なくなった」は，「本をあまり読まないから，知的欲求が少ない」

と解し，just because they read fewer books, they have less thirst for knowledge とする．または，「読書の冊数が少ないため，それだけ知的欲求も少ない」と考え，the＋比較級..., the＋比較級を用いる．つまり，the fewer books they read, the less desire for knowledge they have と訳す．「～と即断しては間違いでしょう」は，it would be a mistake to form the hasty conclusion that ～ または you would be mistaken in jumping to the conclusion that ～ とする

〈解 答 例〉

(i) Some people complain that young people these days read few books, but it would be a mistake to form the hasty conclusion that just because they read fewer books, they have less desire for knowledge.

(ii) People often express regret that young people today don't read many books, but you would be mistaken in jumping to the conclusion that the fewer books they read, the less thirst for knowledge they have.

☆

――〈例題 2〉――
　読書方法にはいろいろあるが，書物はいつでもできる限りゆっくり読むべきである．読み手が時間をかけてゆっくり読まないかぎり，著者の言わんとするところを正しく読みとることはできないだろう．

■[語 句]「できる限りゆっくり読む」read as slowly as possible /「時間をかけて，ゆっくり読む」spend a lot of time in reading a book, take as much time as one can to read a book
■[考え方]「書物はいつでもできる限りゆっくり読むべきである」は，一般の人々を表わす you を主語にし，能動態にするか，books を主語にして受動態にも書くことができる．「読み手」

を a reader とせず，単に you で表わせばよい．「著者の言わんとするところ」は，what an author wants to say，または an author's intention [point of view] などと訳す

〈解　答　例〉

(i)　There are many ways of reading, but books should be read as slowly as possible.　If you don't spend much time in reading a book, it will probably be impossible to correctly understand what its author wants to say.

(ii)　There are various ways of reading, but you should read books as slowly as you can.　Unless you take as much time as you can to read a book, you will fail to grasp its author's point of view properly.

☆

――〈例題 3〉――
　30年近く，ペーパーバックを相手にしてきたが，そんなにたくさん読んでいるわけではない．私は速く読めないので，他人がアメリカのペーパーバックを2, 3時間で1冊読みあげるなどという話を聞くと，とても信じられない．そんなに速く読めるはずはないと思う．

■[語　句]　「ペーパーバック」a paperback /「速く読む」read rapidly, read fast. 名詞表現で，a rapid [fast] reader ともいう /「読みあげる」finish reading from cover to cover, read through
■[考え方]　「30年近く...を相手にしてきた」は，「30年間も...を読んできた」と現在完了進行形を用いる．「ペーパーバックを読み始め，30年近くなる」と解し，It is [has been] almost thirty years since I started reading paperbacks. とも表現できる．「...で1冊読みあげるなどという話を聞くと」の「...という話を聞くと」は省略し，「1冊読みあげられると言

う」と考える．「とても信じられない」は，「彼らが信じられない」と解す

   <　解　答　例　>

(i)　For nearly thirty years I have been reading paperbacks, but I haven't read so many, because I can't read fast. Some people say that they can finish reading an American paperback from cover to cover in two or three hours, but I can't believe them. I think it is impossible for anyone to read at such a pace.

(ii)　It has been almost thirty years since I started reading paperbacks, but I can't say I've read a great deal, since I am not a rapid reader. When I hear someone boast that he can read through an American paperback in a few hours, I can hardly believe him. It can't be true that people can read so rapidly.

☆

─〈例題 4〉─
　外国旅行をするたびに，ぼくは若いときにもっと外国語を勉強しておけばよかったと後悔しないことはない．理想をいえば，どの国に行っても，その言葉が話せるのが望ましい．

■[語 句]　「理想をいえば」ideally speaking, from an idealistic viewpoint

■[考え方]　第1文は，「外国を旅行するたびに，若いとき外国語を熱心に勉強しなかったことをいつも後悔する」と解す．または，「若いとき外国語をもっと勉強しておけばよかったと思わずに，外国旅行はできない」と，二重否定に訳すのもよい．第2文の「その国の言葉が話せるのが望ましい」は，「どこの国に行

っても，そこで話されている言葉を話すことができることが望ましい」とするか，「どこへ行っても，訪ねている国の言葉を話すことができることが望ましいことである」とする．

〈解　答　例〉

(i) Whenever I travel to a foreign country, I regret I did not study foreign languages harder when I was young.　Ideally speaking, it is desirable that, no matter what country you visit, you should be able to speak the language spoken there.

(ii) I never travel abroad without wishing I had studied foreign languages harder in my youth.　From an idealistic viewpoint, it is to be desired that, wherever we go, we should learn to speak the language of the foreign country we are visiting.

☆

──〈例題 5〉──
　この頃，日本では新婚さんが新婚旅行で外国に出かけることが流行している．しかし，言葉が問題となり，旅行中，日本で習った英語を使っても，話が通じなくて大変苦労している．

■[語　句]　「新婚さん」newly-married couples, newly weds /「新婚旅行」one's honeymoon /「流行している」fashionable, popular /「話が通じなくて苦労する」find it difficult to communicate, have difficulty (in) expressing oneself

■[考え方]　第1文は，形式主語 it を用い，「新婚旅行のため外国に出かけること」を不定詞で表わし，It is fashionable...to go to foreign countries for one's honeymoon. とする．「新婚旅行」には必ず人称代名詞の所有格を前につけることに注意する．不定詞の意味上の主語である「新婚さん」は，前置詞 for

を用い，どこに置いたらよいか？「新婚旅行で海外に行くこと」を動名詞で表わし，補語に popular を用いれば，解答例 (ii) の英文ができる．「言葉が問題となる」は，「彼らは言語で問題にぶつかる」と解し，they run into problems with the language とする．または，「彼らが取り組まねばならぬ問題は言語である」と考え，the problem they have to tackle is the language ともできる．「日本で習った英語を使っても」は，「日本(の学校)で習った種類の英語を使う」と解し，use the kind of English they learned at school in Japan とする．「～使っても」の部分を譲歩構文で表わすのもよい

〈 解 答 例 〉

(i) These days in Japan it is fashionable for newly-married couples to go to foreign countries for their honeymoon. Sometimes, however, they run into problems with the language while traveling, and find it difficult to communicate with the people there, using the kind of English they learned at school in Japan.

(ii) Going overseas on their honeymoon is popular with newly-weds these days in Japan. However, the problem they have to tackle while traveling is the language, and they often have great difficulty (in) expressing themselves, no matter how hard they try to use the type of English they learned in Japan.

第11章
文化・芸術・科学

Check & Check

□豊かな文化遺産を後世に伝える ⇨ hand down a rich cultural heritage to posterity
　▶heritage の代わりに，inheritance も用いられる
□国家間の文化交流 ⇨ a cultural exchange between [among] nations
□文化の進んだ国[民] ⇨ a cultured nation
　▶「文化的国民」⇨ a cultural nation /「文化活動」⇨ cultural activities /「文化人」⇨ a man of culture, a cultured man
□文化の高い[低い]国 ⇨ a nation of high [low] culture
　▶culture は「精神文化」を，civilization は「物質文化」，つまり「文明」を意味する
□人類の文化水準を高める ⇨ raise the cultural level of the

第11章　文化・芸術・科学

human race
- □文化施設 ⇨ cultural facilities [institutions]
- □国宝 ⇨ a national treasure
  - ▶「重要文化財」⇨ an important cultural asset
- □文化祭を行なう ⇨ hold a cultural festival
  - ▶「文化祭を祝う」は，celebrate a festival という
- □文化が進む[退歩する] ⇨ advance [retrograde] in civilization
- □先進国 ⇨ an advanced [a developed] country
  - ▶「工業先進国」⇨ an industrially advanced country /「発展途上国」⇨ a developing country
- □西洋の思想を日本に輸入する ⇨ introduce Western ideas into Japan
- □中国文化は日本文化に非常に大きな影響を及ぼした ⇨ Chinese culture has had a very great influence on Japanese culture.
  - ▶influence は，不可算名詞だが，前に形容詞がくるとよく不定冠詞 a を伴う．have an effect on ～ も同義
- □文明の進歩 ⇨ the progress of civilization
  - ▶「文明が進むにつれて」⇨ as civilization advances [progresses, makes progress]
  - ▶「進歩する」の次の名詞の同意表現 (a), (b), (c) に注意
    - (a)「彼の英語は非常に進歩している」⇨ He is making good *progress* in his English.
    - (b)「科学は今世紀，めざましく進歩している」⇨ Science has made remarkable *advances* in this century.
    - (c)「日本経済は1960年代に急速な発展を示した」⇨ Japan's economy showed rapid *development* in the 1960's.

つまり，これらの表現の progress, development は通例，形容詞をつけ，無冠詞．advance は複数形で用いられる

☐外国文化を取り入れ，自分自身のものにする ⇨ adopt a foreign culture and make it one's own

☐独自の文明を開発する ⇨ develop a civilization of its own

☐彼らは背後に長い歴史を有している ⇨ They have a long history behind them.

☐文学はことばの芸術である ⇨ Literature is a work of art with words.

☐日本人の文学を西洋に紹介する ⇨ interpret the literature of the Japanese people to the Western world

☐彼はフランス文学の研究に専念した ⇨ He devoted himself to the study of French literature.
▶devote oneself to の to は前置詞

☐それぞれの国のことばは，一国の文化や国民性の反映である ⇨ Each language reflects the culture and character of the nation that uses it.

☐彼は文化勲章を受けた ⇨ He was awarded a Cultural Medal.
▶be awarded の代わりに，receive, win なども用いられる

☐自然[応用]科学 ⇨ natural [applied] science

☐技術水準 ⇨ the level of technology
▶「技術刷新」⇨ technological innovation

☐自然現象 ⇨ a natural phenomenon
▶「自然の法則」⇨ a law of nature, a natural law

☐科学技術 ⇨ science and technology
▶technology だけで，「科学技術」の意にも用いられる．「高

第11章 文化・芸術・科学

度先端技術」⇨ high technology
- □科学の産業への応用 ⇨ the application of science to industry
  - ▶「科学的発見を生産方法に応用する」⇨ apply scientific discoveries to industrial production methods
- □アメリカによって打ち上げられた通信衛星は，オリンピックのテレビ中継に大いに使用された ⇨ The communications satellite launched by the U.S. was largely used for relaying the TV broadcast of the Olympic Games.
- □日本は気象衛星の打ち上げに成功した ⇨ Japan has succeeded in launching a weather satellite.
- □実用放送衛星 ⇨ a practical television broadcasting satellite
- □地球物理学[者] ⇨ geophysics [geophysicist]
  - ▶「生化学[者]」⇨ biochemistry [biochemist] /「原子物理学[者]」⇨ nuclear physics [nuclear physicist]
- □半導体 ⇨ semiconductor
  - ▶「(熱・電気・音の) 伝導体」⇨ conductor /「水は電気をよく伝える」⇨ Water is a good conductor of electricity.
- □科学が万能だと考える者がいる ⇨ Some people think that science is everything.
  - ▶「万能」を文字通り，almighty とか，omnipotent とするのは誤り．なお，英語では，「全能の神」を the Almighty God という
- □中国は自国の豊かな天然資源を開発している ⇨ China is developing its ample natural resources.
  - ▶resource は「資源」の意では，複数形
- □この国は鉱物資源に富む ⇨ This country is rich in mineral

resources.
- □資源を愛護する ⇨ conserve [economize] resources
  - ▶「(自然及び資源の)保護論者」⇨ conservationist
- □エネルギーの浪費はやがて石油資源を枯渇させるだろう ⇨ Waste of energy will eventually drain resources.
- □省エネする ⇨ cut down on energy costs
  - ▶単に save energy costs ともいう
- □宇宙飛行士たちは月の探検をした ⇨ The astronauts made explorations of the moon.
  - ▶動詞表現：The astronauts explored the moon.
- □いつの日か，宇宙旅行で月に行けるでしょう ⇨ Someday we will be able to travel through space to the moon.
  - ▶この表現では，space は無冠詞
- □原子力時代 ⇨ the atomic [nuclear] age
  - ▶「宇宙時代」⇨ the age of space science
- □原子力を平和目的に利用する ⇨ use nuclear energy for peaceful purposes
- □核戦争[兵器] ⇨ a nuclear war [weapon]
- □原子力潜水艦 ⇨ a nuclear-powered submarine
- □原子力発電所 ⇨ a nuclear power plant [station]
- □原水爆禁止世界会議 ⇨ World Conference Against Atomic and Hydrogen Bombs
- □戦略核戦力 ⇨ strategic nuclear forces
- □米ロ中距離核戦力全廃に合意 ⇨ the US-Russia agreement to eliminate INF [*I*ntermediate-range *N*uclear *F*orces]
- □放射性降下物退避所 ⇨ a fallout shelter

第11章　文化・芸術・科学

☐日本製のトランジスタ・ラジオは世界中で知られている ⇨ Japanese-made transistor radios are known all over the world.

☐この小型の電卓は，ポケットに携行するのに便利です ⇨ This small-size electronic calculator is convenient for carrying in the pocket.
　▶小型のものを特に，a calculating machine という

☐電気を起こすのに水力を利用する ⇨ use water to generate electricity

☐電気がどんなに早く伝わるかわかりますか ⇨ Can you tell how fast electricity travels?

☐この科学の時代でも，よく観察すると，人が考えているより多くの事柄が迷信に左右されている ⇨ Even in this age of science, a careful look will show us that more things than we might think are affected [influenced] by superstition.
　▶superstition は，可算名詞として複数にもなる

☐当工場でロボットを使用すると，大量の失業者がでると恐れられている ⇨ They are afraid that the use of robots in this factory will cause [lead to] a large increase in unemployment.
　▶「大量の失業者がでる」は ～ will cause large-scale unemployment ともいえる

☐科学の育成強化 ⇨ the cultivation and promotion of science

☐われわれは化学の実験をしている ⇨ We are making [carrying out, performing] an experiment in chemistry.
　▶動詞表現：We are experimenting in chemistry.

Let's Try

【I】 次の文中の(   )内に与えられている語から，適当なものを選び，日本文の意味になるようにしなさい．

1. That professor has devoted his life to (study, the study, studying) nuclear physics.
(その教授は原子物理学の研究に生涯をささげた)
2. This book gives a good (information, picture, images) of life and culture in Japan 200 years ago.
(この本は200年前における日本の生活と文化をよく描写している)
3. Jones had no formal school education, but he was well (cultured, known, mannered).
(ジョーンズは正式な学校教育を受けていないが，教養があった)
4. The Englishman has a good (skill, information, knowledge) of Japanese literature.
(そのイギリス人は日本文学によく通じている)
5. There have been great (advances, progress, development) in space travel in the last 30 years.
(過去30年間に宇宙旅行が大きく進歩してきた)

■[ヒント] 1. devote one's life to の to は不定詞の to か，前置詞の to か． 2. information「知識」は不可算名詞． 3.「教養がある人」は a man of culture. 4.「よく通じている」は be well versed in ともいう． have a good (   ) of の表現は，know の名詞形を補う． 5. There have been ～ は，複数形の主語が期待される．

■[解答] 1. studying 2. picture 3. cultured 4. knowledge 5. advances

第 11 章　文化・芸術・科学

【II】 日本文の意味に合うように（　　）内の語句を並べ換えなさい.

1. 私は博物館で美術品を眺めて終日過ごした.
   (the works, in the museum, the entire day, spent, of art, looking, I, at)
2. だれもが宇宙旅行できる時代がやがて来るだろう.
   (The time, not, will be able to, anybody, is, probably, travel, when, far off, in space)
3. その画家は妻の精神的援助をえて, 大作を描き上げた.
   (the masterpiece, his wife, completed, the moral support, with, that artist, of)
4. 私は学校の代表として英語弁論大会に出たが, 入賞しなかった.
   (the English speech contest, a prize, our school, in, represented, failed, I, to win, but)
5. アメリカに行って, われわれの文化と違っていることを実感した.
   (realize, to America, different, was, went, was from ours, able to, and, their culture, how, I)

■[ヒント]　**1.**「眺めて…過ごす」は spend＋時間＋〜ing 形の文型で.　**2.**「旅行できる時代」は the time when とし, when の形容詞節は, 未来時制で. far off は distant の意.　**4.**「英語弁論大会で, 学校を代表した」と解す.「入賞しない」は, fail to 〜 で.　**5.**「彼らの文化がわれわれの文化と違っていることを実感する」と解し, realize how＋形容詞＋S＋V の文型を用いる

■[解答]　**1.** I spent the entire day looking at the works of art in the museum.　**2.** The time when anybody will be able to travel in space is probably not far off.　**3.** That artist completed the masterpiece with the moral support of his wife.

4. I represented our school in the English speech contest, but failed to win a prize.   5. I went to America and was able to realize how different their culture was from ours.

Let's Memorize

1. 重要文化財は大切に保存しなければならない.

   Important cultural treasures must be carefully preserved.

2. パリで絵を学びたいという長年の彼の希望がやっとかなった.

   His long cherished hope of studying painting in Paris finally came true.

3. この著作で彼は偉大な小説家として名声をあげた.

   This work established his fame as a great novelist.

4. 彼女は世界的に有名な先生に声楽を習っている.

   She is taking vocal lessons from a world-famous teacher.

5. あの米国人は日本美術に通じている.

   The American has a thorough knowledge of Japanese art.

6. 新聞やテレビで世界中の出来事を知ることができる.

   Newspapers and television keep us informed of world events.

7. このテレビは調子が悪い.

   This TV set isn't working very well.

8. 宇宙旅行の実現はまだ遠い.

   It will still be a long time before traveling in outer space becomes a reality.

9. コンピューターの発明で現代の社会は大きく変わっ

   The invention of the computer has greatly changed

第11章 文化・芸術・科学

た．

10. ヘンリーからパソコンの操作を説明してもらったが，ややこしくて分からなかった．

11. スイスの精密機械工業は，その技術で世界に高い評判を得ている．

12. もし核戦争が起こったとしたら，人類は生き残れるかどうか分からない．

13. 核兵器の生産は世界の平和を危くする．

14. この世から核兵器をなくす方法はないだろうか．

15. 医学は年々進歩しつつある．

present-day society.

Henry explained to me how to operate a personal computer but it was so complicated that I didn't understand too well.

Switzerland's precision machinery industry has a high reputation for technology all over the world.

No one can tell whether the human race could survive if a nuclear war were to break out.

The production of nuclear weapons causes danger to world peace.

Isn't there a way to eliminate nuclear weapons from the world?

Medical science continues to make progress year by year.

Exercises

〈例題 1〉

科学技術の長足な発達によって，人間は物質的な豊かさを享受することができるようになったが，反面，科学が必ずしも人間の幸福を増進させないこともわかってきた．

■[語句] 「科学技術」science and technology /「物質的な豊かさ」material prosperity

■[考え方] 「～の発達によって，人間は物質的な豊かさを享受する」は，次の2通りが考えられる．1つは，「科学技術のおかげで，人間は物質的に豊かである」と解し，もう1つは，「科学技術の長足な発達」を主語にし，「人間が物質的豊かさを受けることを可能にした」とする．後者は, Great progress in technology has made it possible for [enabled] human beings to enjoy material prosperity. となる．これは無生物主語による頻出構文．「科学が必ずしも人間の幸福を増進させない」は，部分否定に注意し, science does not necessarily make people happy, または science does not always promote the welfare of people とする

〈解　答　例〉

(i) Due to great progress in science and technology, people are materially rich, but they have realized that science does not always make them happy.

(ii) Great developments in technology have make it possible for human beings to enjoy material prosperity, but, on the other hand, they have become aware that science does not necessarily promote their welfare.

☆

┌──〈例題 2〉──
│　最近コンピューターがいろいろな分野に応用され，日本語を英語に訳す機械も開発されている．しかし，複雑な文章は無理で，翻訳家にとって代わるのにはまだ当分かかるでしょう．
└──

■[語句] 「コンピューター」computers /「翻訳家」translators
■[考え方] 「日本語を英語に訳す機械も開発されている」は，

第11章 文化・芸術・科学

「日本語を英語に直す機械 (machines with which to turn Japanese into English) も開発されている」または，「和英翻訳機械 (Japanese-English translating machines) も考案されている」と解す.「翻訳家にとって代わるのにはまだ当分かかるでしょう」は，It will be a long time [some time] before... の構文を用い，before 以下は「これらの機械が人間の翻訳家の代わりをする」の意の副詞節とする.

〈解　答　例〉

(i) Recently computers have been used in many fields, and machines with which to turn Japanese into English, have been devised as well.　However, they can't translate complicated sentences.　It will be some time before they can replace translators.

(ii) Computers have been applied to various fields recently, and Japanese-English translating machines have been invented.　But it is difficult for them to handle intricate sentences, and it will be a long time before they can take the place of human translators.

☆

――〈例題 3〉――
　ヨーロッパの会社では，主として失業者が多数でると恐れられ，ロボットが敬遠されているそうだ．確かに，ロボットが人間よりも勝れたことができるとしても，人間がその支配に屈することはあってはならぬ．

■[語　句]　「失業者」jobless people, unemployed people /「ロボット」industrial robots
■[考え方]　第1文は「失業者がたくさんでると思われるので，ヨーロッパの会社はロボットを使用することを避けている」と訳す．「避ける」avoid は，動名詞を従えることに注意．

ここを「ロボットの使用が，失業の増加を起こすと心配され，ヨーロッパの会社はロボットの使用を躊躇(ちゅうちょ)している」と解してもよい．第2文は，「確かにロボットが人間よりもよい仕事をする場合もあるが，人間はロボットに支配されてはならない」と考えるか，「たとえ，ロボットが多くの点で勝れていても，人間はロボットに劣ってしまってはならぬ」と解す．

〈解　答　例〉

(i) People say that companies in Europe avoid using industrial robots, mainly because they are afraid that this will result in many people losing their jobs. In some cases it is true that robots can do a better job than humans, but people should not allow themselves to be controlled by robots.

(ii) It is said that European companies hesitate to use robots, chiefly because they are worried that the use of robots will cause a large increase in unemployment. Human beings, however, should never permit themselves to *become second to* robots, even if robots are superior in many respects.

▶become second to は become inferior to ～「～に劣る」の意

☆

―〈例題 4〉――
　一般に日本人は，日本のことよりも外国のことやその文化にとても詳しい．これは，日本が外国の文化を取り入れることに熱心だったが，日本のことを外国に説明することにはあまり熱意をもたなかったことに一因がある．

■[語　句]「一般に」in general, generally /「日本のこと」things Japanese, things about Japan /「外国の文化を取り入れる」adopt foreign cultures

第11章　文化・芸術・科学

■[考え方]　「日本人は...とても詳しい」は,「日本人は...よく知っている」と直す.「これは...に一因がある」は, In part, this is because... または This is due partly to the fact that... とする.「日本が外国の文化を取り入れることに熱心だったが, 日本のことを外国に説明することにはあまり熱意をもたなかった」は,「日本人は, 日本のことを外国人に説明するよりも, 外国の文化を日本に紹介することに強い興味をもっていた」と解す.

〈解　答　例〉

(i)　In general, Japanese people know more about other countries and cultures than about Japan. In part, this is because Japanese people have been more keenly interested in introducing foreign cultures into Japan than explaining things Japanese to foreign people.

(ii)　Generally speaking, the average Japanese person is more knowledgeable about foreign countries and cultures than about Japan. This is due partly to the fact that Japan has been very enthusiastic about adopting foreign cultures, but not so eager to make itself known to foreign countries.

☆

――〈例題 5〉――
日本語は現在のところ世界の言語の中で孤立している. このことは日本人にどんな影響を与えているであろうか. まず, 英語, ドイツ語, フランス語などと著しく違うために, これらの外国語を習得する上で, 種々不都合なことが多い. 一方, 他国人に日本文化を知ってもらう場合の障害の大きさは予想以上である.

■[語　句]　「影響」an influence /「障害」an obstacle

■[考え方]「世界の言語の中で孤立している」は,「世界の他の言語から孤立している」と解す.「このことが日本人にどんな影響を与えているか」は, have an influence on または動詞 affect を用いる.「英語, ドイツ語, フランス語などと著しく違うために, これらの外国語を習得する上で...不都合なことが多い」は,「英語, ドイツ語, フランス語などの外国語を学ぶとき, われわれは非常に不利である. なぜならば, これらの外国語が日本語と全く違うからだ」とするか,「日本語と英語, ドイツ語, フランス語のような言語の間には, 大きな相違があるので, われわれがこれらの外国語を学ぶときは, 不利な立場にある」と解す.「不利な立場にある」は at a disadvantage か, in an unfavorable position などの熟語を用いる. 最後の,「障害の大きさは予想以上である」は,「彼らが直面しなければならぬ困難は, 予想以上に大きい」か,「外国人が克服しなければならぬ障害は, 思ったより重大である」と考える.

〈 解 答 例 〉

(i) Japanese is now isolated from the other languages of the world. What kind of influence does this fact have on the Japanese people? In the first place, we are at a great disadvantage when learning foreign languages, such as English, German, and French, because they are entirely different from Japanese. On the other hand, when foreign people try to study Japanese culture, the difficulties that they have to face are greater than they first expected.

(ii) Japanese stands apart from the other languages of the world. How does this affect the Japanese people? First, since there are considerable differences between Japanese and such languages as English, German, and French, we are in an unfavorable position when studying these foreign languages.　On the other hand, the obstacles that foreign people have to overcome when they are trying to study Japanese culture, are often more serious than they first expected.

第12章
教育・勉強・学校

Check & Check

□久美はアメリカで大学教育を受けた ⇨ Kumi had a college education in the United States.
　▶education は，不可算名詞．しかし，前に修飾語がつくと不定冠詞 a をつける．動詞表現：Kumi was educated at a college in the United States.

□父は貧しかったが，私に立派な教育を受けさせてくれた ⇨ My father was poor, but gave me a good education.

□小学校 ⇨ an elementary [a primary] school
　▶「中学校」⇨ a junior high school /「高校」⇨ a senior high school /「中等教育」⇨ secondary education

□きみは今学期は，どんな学科を取っているか ⇨ What subjects are you taking this semester?

第12章　教育・勉強・学校

▶「必修科目」⇨ a required subject /「選択科目」⇨ an elective subject

□この大学では，英語で授業を行なう ⇨ In this college we conduct lessons in English.
　▶この場合，lesson は複数形

□明日の予習をしましたか ⇨ Did you prepare your lessons for tomorrow?
　▶この表現も，lesson は複数形が多い

□自分の勉強を怠ける ⇨ neglect one's lessons

□彼の息子は学校の成績がいい[悪い] ⇨ His son does well [poorly] at school.

□悠太君はいつも数学で良い点をとります ⇨ Yuta always gets [receives] good marks in mathematics.
　▶「〜で良い[満]点をとる」は，get good [full] marks in 〜 と複数形で，get a good grade in 〜 と，単数形も同義の表現

□明日，物理の試験がある ⇨ We have an examination in physics tomorrow.
　▶have a test in 〜 も同義の表現

□彼は来年大学入試を受ける ⇨ He will take a college entrance examination next year.
　▶「大学入試を受ける」を He will sit for a college entrance examination. ともいう

□試験に首尾よく合格する ⇨ pass an examination successfully

□歴史の試験に落第する ⇨ fail (in) the history examination

□彼は入学試験の準備を始めた ⇨ He began to prepare for the entrance examination.

□太郎は大学に進学することを真剣に考えている ⇨ Taro is seriously considering the idea of going to college.
　▶「大学に進学する」は go to (a) university ともいう

□入試の結果が今日発表になり，約300名がこの大学に入学を許可された ⇨ The results of the entrance examination were published today, and about three hundred students were admitted to this college.

□高校時代に，彼はたくさんの課外活動に参加した ⇨ He took part in a lot of extra-curricular activities when he was in high school.
　▶この take part in は be engaged in ともいえる

□今晩は宿題をやらねばなりません ⇨ I have to do my homework this evening.
　▶study my homework は誤り

□その子は宿題をやってこなかったことで，先生に叱られるのをこわがっている ⇨ The child is afraid of being scolded by the teacher for not having done his homework.
　▶for 以下を, for failing to do his homework としてもよい

□私たちの高校は，丘の上にあり，町の美しい全景が見渡せる ⇨ Our high school is on a hill affording [commanding] a beautiful view of the whole city.
　▶「景色を見渡す」の次の表現 (a), (b) に注意しよう．
　　(a)「この窓から湖の景色がよく見える」⇨ This window affords [commands, gives] a fine view of the lake.
　　(b)「うちのアパートから富士山がよく見える」⇨ We can get a good view of Mt. Fuji from our apartment.
　　　主語が, (a) は無生物, (b) は人間

□私たちの学校は駅から10分ばかり歩いたところにあります ⇨

第12章　教育・勉強・学校

Our school is about a ten-minute walk from the station.
▶この表現を, within a ten minutes' walk of the station ともいえる. within ～ のときは of になるのが慣用

□新学期は **4月10日**から始まる ⇒ The new term begins [starts] on April 10.
▶「4月10日から」を, on the tenth of April ともいう.「～から」を from としないこと
▶「授業は8時半から始まる」⇒ School begins [starts] at 8:30. (eight-thirty と読む)

□君はどこの学校へ行っているの ⇒ What school do you attend [go to]?
▶「(授業を受けに)学校へ行く」の意のときは無冠詞

□明日は授業があるの ⇒ Do you have school tomorrow?
▶Do you have any classes tomorrow? も同義

□きのう三郎は病気で英語の授業を休んだ ⇒ Saburo missed the English class yesterday because he was sick.
▶「授業をさぼる」は cut [skip] class, または play truant などという

□学校はいつから夏休みですか ⇒ When does your school break up for the summer vacation?
▶When do you break up for the summer vacation? ともいう. break up は「休暇などで授業が終わり, 一時的に解散する」の意

□「2時間目は何の授業ですか」「英語だよ」⇒ "What do we have in the second period?" "We have English."

□日本の教育制度はアメリカの教育制度と, かなりちがっている ⇒ The Japanese educational system is considerably different from that of the United States.

□ジェリーは奨学金をもらって大学へ進学した ⇨ Jerry got [received, won] a scholarship to go to college.
　▶この表現では，scholarship は不定冠詞 a とともに用いる. cf.「彼は英文学に造詣(ぞうけい)の深い人である」⇨ He is a man of profound scholarship in English literature. scholarship「学識」の意のときは，無冠詞

□アメリカでは，大学に入るのはやさしいが，入ってからむずかしい ⇨ In America it is easy to get into college but difficult to stay there [in college].

□兄は健康上の理由で，16歳のときに学校をやめねばならなかった ⇨ My brother had to leave school at the age of 16 for health reasons.
　▶leave school は「退学する」の意であるが，「学校を卒業する」の意のときもある

□彼は1980年にオックスフォードを優等で卒業した ⇨ He graduated from Oxford with honors in 1980.
　▶graduate は英国では，学位を取って大学を卒業する意. 米国では，大学以外の各種の学校を卒業するときにも用いる

□トムのような立派な生徒は，わが校の名誉となります ⇨ A good student like Tom does [brings] honor to our school.
　▶do honor to ～ は do ～ honor としてもよい. cf.「わが校はトムを大いに誇りにしている」⇨ Tom is a great honor to our school. この honor は，不定冠詞を伴う

□彼の悪い振舞いは，わが校の名を汚した ⇨ His bad behavior brought shame [disgrace] on our school.
　▶bring shame on は，bring shame to ともいう. cf. 彼は両親の面汚しだ ⇨ He is a shame [a disgrace] to his parents. 冠詞に注意

第12章　教育・勉強・学校

- □君が英語の試験でよくなかったとは残念だ ⇨ It's a shame that you did a poor job in your English exam.
  - ▶この表現は, It is a pity [too bad] that ～ と同義
- □少年は歴史の試験でカンニングしたことを恥ずかしく思った ⇨ The boy felt shame at having cheated on [in] the history examination.
  - ▶be ashamed of を用いて, The boy was ashamed of having cheated on [in] the history examination. も同義の表現
- □彼は法律を専攻している ⇨ He majors in law.
  - ▶He is a law major. ともいう. 英国では, specialize in を使う
- □鈴木さんはテキサス大学で学位を取りました ⇨ Miss Suzuki got [took, received] her degree at the University of Texas.
- □加藤氏はコロムビア大学から文学修士の学位を受けている ⇨ Mr. Kato has [holds] an M.A. degree from Columbia University.
  - ▶an M.A. degree は, the Master of Arts degree ともいう
- □入学志願者 ⇨ an applicant [a candidate] (for admission)
  - ▶「入学願書」 ⇨ an application for admission
- □願書を提出する ⇨ send in an application
- □学費に困る ⇨ be hard up for school expenses
- □私たちは, そのインドの学生の学費を出してやることに決めた ⇨ We have decided to pay for the Indian student's college education.
  - ▶pay for his college education は, pay his expenses while at college ともいえる
- □一郎の両親は息子を大学にやるだけの経済的余裕がなかっ

□た ⇨ Ichiro's parents couldn't afford the expense of sending him to college.

□彼は私費でアメリカに留学した ⇨ He studied in the United States at his own expense.

□子供2人を大学にやるのは，私にかなりの出費だった ⇨ Sending two children to college put me to considerable expense.
　▶put someone to expense は，「人に金を使わせる」の意．この expense は無冠詞

□わざわざ金をかけて，個人教授を受けるのはばかげている ⇨ It is ridiculous [silly] to go to the expense of taking private lessons.
　▶go to the expense of ～ing は，「金をかけて～する」の意．この expense は定冠詞をつけて用いる

□大学生活を楽しむ ⇨ enjoy one's college life

□校内暴力 ⇨ school [campus] violence
　▶campus violence は主として大学の場合に用いられる

□この一週間，私たちのクラスは全員出席です ⇨ Our class has had perfect attendance for the past week.
　▶この attendance は無冠詞

□その子は学校にきちんと出席するが，勉強に精を出さない ⇨ The child attends school regularly, but never attends to his school work.
　▶「出席する」attend は他動詞，「～に身を入れる」attend to ～ は自動詞

□わが高校の創立百周年記念式典は10月10日に挙行される ⇨ The centennial celebration of our high school is to be held on October 10.

▶to be held を to take place ともいえる
▶「わが校は創立50周年祭を11月3日に祝う」⇒ Our school will celebrate the 50th anniversary of its founding on November 3.

Let's Try

【 I 】 次の英文 (a) (b) の意味が等しくなるように，(b) の空所に適当な語を補いなさい．
1. (a) His son was educated in college in Paris.
   (b) His son had a (　　) (　　) in Paris.
2. (a) Emily was successful in the final examination.
   (b) Emily (　　) (　　) in the final examination.
3. (a) You may find it difficult to get good marks in every subject.
   (b) You may find (　　) in (　　) good marks in every subject.
4. (a) Junko's favorite subject is English.
   (b) Junko is (　　) (　　) English.
5. (a) That child is so energetic that he doesn't keep still a moment.
   (b) That child is (　　) energetic (　　) keep still a moment.

■[ヒント] 1.「大学教育を受けた」の意． 2.「期末試験がよくできた」の意． 3. difficult を名詞形に，get を動名詞に変え名詞構文にする． 4.「得意である」の意． 5.「元気で片ときもじっとしていない」の意

■[解 答] 1. college education　2. did well　3. difficulty, getting　4. good at　5. too, to

【II】 次の英文が，和文の意味になるように，空所に与えられている語句の中から最も適当なものを選びなさい．
1. 彼はとうとうクラスの同窓会に来なかった．
Eventually he didn't show up at the class (party, meeting, reunion).
2. 子供を無理に勉強させるのはかわいそうです．
I feel sorry for children who are (encouraged, allowed, forced) to study.
3. テレビがついていると気が散って勉強ができない．
I get (distracted, worried, excited) and can't study when the television is on.
4. どの生徒もこの問題が解けなかった．
(Neither, None, Nobody) of the students could solve this problem.
5. 試験のヤマがはずれて，全くできなかった．
I guessed wrong about what would be in the examination, and (did, failed, made) very badly.

■[ヒント] 1. 卒業後のクラス会は，「再会の集い」とする． 2.「強制される」の意． 3.「気が散る」は attract の反対． 4. Neither は生徒が2人，None は3人以上のグループの場合に用いられる． 5. failed ならば, very badly は不必要．「良い成績だった」は did well という

■[解答] 1. reunion 2. forced 3. distracted 4. None 5. did

【III】 次の各文を文尾の（　　）内の指示に従って書き換えなさい．
1. She is a teacher rather than a scholar.
　　　　　　　　　　(She is not で始める)
2. Mr. Hayashi teaches history in a local school.
　　　　　　　　　　(動詞を be 動詞にして)

第12章　教育・勉強・学校

■[ヒント]　1.「...というよりはむしろ～」という表現のもう1つの言い方．　2.「～の先生である」とする

■[解答]　1. She is not so much a scholar as a teacher.　2. Mr. Hayashi is a history teacher [a teacher of history] in a local school.

Let's Memorize

1. 僕は高校入学以来，一日も欠席していない．

   I haven't missed a single day since entering high school.

2. 私は勉強するのに，よく大学図書館を利用します．

   I often make use of the university library to study.

3. ほかの科目は不得意だが，数学だけは自信がある．

   I am poor at all other subjects, but I'm confident in math.

4. 期末試験では，英語が特に悪かった．

   In the final examinations, I did an especially poor job in English.

5. 試験の結果は予想以上に良かった．

   The results of the examination were better than I (had) expected.

6. 姉は試験の準備で忙しい．

   My sister is very busy preparing for her examination.

7. 昨夜は，2時まで起きて，試験勉強した．

   Last night I stayed up till two o'clock studying for the examination.

8. 幸いにも，私たちはクラブ活動を通じて親しくなった．

   It was fortunate that we became acquainted with each other through club activities.

9. 勉強ばかりしてないで，たまには気晴らしに出かけろよ．	Go out and have a good time once in a while instead of just studying all the time.
10. 彼女はできの悪い息子のことでいつもこぼしている．	She is always complaining about her son doing badly at school.
11. 先週はのんびりしたから，やらねばならぬことがたくさんある．	Last week I took it easy, so there are a lot of things I've got to do.
12. 学校の勉強が社会ですぐ役立つとは限らない．	What is learned at school isn't always immediately useful in society.
13. 彼の大学における学業はぐんぐん進歩した．	He has made rapid progress in his studies at the university.
14. 近い将来，機会をつかみ，留学したいと思っている．	I hope I can get the chance to study abroad in the near future.
15. 彼女は教育の仕事に深い興味をもっている．	She takes a deep interest in her work in education.

Exercises

──〈例題 1〉──
　本に書いてあることは学校に行けば覚えられるが，人間性については，学校ではあまり学ぶことができない．自分のうちと学校を往復しているだけで，人間ができるように思うのは甘い考えだ．

■[語句]「人間性」human nature /「学校を往復する」go to and from school /「甘い考え」an optimistic idea

■[考え方]「本に書いてあることは学校に行けば覚えられる」は,「本の中に書かれていることは学校で覚えられる」と解し,You can learn in school what books say [what is written in books]. とする.「自分のうちと学校を往復しているだけで,人間ができる」は,「学校を往復することだけで,君の人格が形成される助けとなる」と考えるか,「われわれの人柄が学校に出席することによってのみ,形成される」と解する.「～と思うのは甘い考えだ」は,It is too simple to think that ～ とも表わせる.

〈解　答　例〉

(i)　You can learn in school what books say, but you cannot learn much about human nature in school. It is too simple to think that merely going to and from school will help you develop your character.

(ii)　We can learn at school what is written in books, but we can never learn much about human nature at school. It is an optimistic idea to think that our character is formed only by attending school.

☆

———〈例題 2〉———
「日本の子供たちは,先生が黒板に書いたことを写しているだけで,その内容については深く考えないね」「君が日本の学校について批判すると,私はふさいだ気分になります」

■[語句]「写す」copy /「その内容」the content /「批判する」criticize /「ふさいだ気分になる」get depressed, feel sad

■[考え方]「その内容については深く考えないね」は,「それがどういう意味かを深く考えずに」と解し,前置詞 without を

用い，副詞句を作る．つまり，without thinking deeply about what it means とする．「君が日本の学校について批判すると，私はふさいだ気分になる」は，「批判するのを聞くと，私は悲しくなる」と単文で表現する．

〈 解 答 例 〉

(i) "Children in Japan only try to copy what their teacher writes on the blackboard without thinking deeply about the content." "When you criticize Japanese schools, I really get depressed."

(ii) "All that Japanese children do in the classroom is just (to) copy down what their teacher writes on the blackboard. They hardly consider what it means, do they?" "Well, it makes me very sad to hear you talk critically about schools in Japan."

☆

〈例題 3〉

　今日，学校では先生が学生に対してあまりにも親切で，なんでもかんでも教えすぎるきらいがある．そこで学生は教えてもらうことに慣れて，自分では勉強しなくなってしまう．もし先生ができるだけ教えまいとし，学生は何とかして先生から学びとろうとするのであれば，教育成果がずいぶんあがるであろう．

■[語 句]　「～に慣れる」get used to ～ /「教育成果」(an) educational effect [results]

■[考え方]　「先生が学生に対してあまりにも親切で，なんでもかんでも教えすぎるきらいがある」は，「先生が学生のためにあまりに尽くし，ほとんどあらゆることを教える傾向にある」と考える．または，so ～ that... の構文を用いてもよい．「そこで...に慣れて，自分では勉強しなくなってしまう」は，

第12章　教育・勉強・学校

「自発的に (on one's own, of one's own accord) 勉強しないのは，学生が教えられることに慣れているからだ」と解し，It is because...that ～ の強調構文を用いる．最後の文は，「先生はできるだけ少なく教えようとし，学生はできるだけ多く学ぶことに努めれば，大きな教育成果が生まれるであろう」と解し，仮定法も用いられる．

〈解　答　例〉

(ⅰ)　Today, teachers do too much for their students; they teach their students almost everything. Therefore, students get so used to being taught that they lose interest in studying on their own. If teachers try to teach as little as they can, and students try to learn as much as they can from their teachers, it will produce greater educational results.

(ⅱ)　In schools today, teachers do so much for their students that they tend to teach their students almost everything. It is because students are accustomed to being taught by teachers that they don't learn of their own accord. If teachers were to teach as little as possible and students to try to learn as much as possible from their teachers, a greater educational effect would be achieved.

☆

───〈例題 4〉───
　私の小学生のころは，勉強よりも遊び相手とけんかをするのが楽しみで学校へ行ったものだ．毎日のように傷を作って帰ってきたが，泣いて帰らぬかぎり，叱られたことなど一度もなかった．

■[語句]「遊び相手」a playmate, a playfellow /「けんかをする」have fights, have scuffles /「傷」a scratch (かき傷), a cut (切り傷), a bruise (打撲傷)

■[考え方]「勉強よりもけんかをするのが楽しみで学校へ行った」は, I went to school, looking forward more to having fights with my playmates than to studying とするか,「私が楽しんだのは, そこで勉強したことよりもむしろ...けんかをしたことだ」と解し, it ~ that... の強調構文を用いる. つまり, it was not so much what I studied there that amused me, as the scuffles I had with my playfellows とする.「毎日のように傷を作って帰ってきた」は,「ほとんど毎日, 新しい傷をつけ, 帰宅した」とし,「傷を作って」は with new scratches か, with cuts and bruises と複数形を用いる

〈解 答 例〉

(i) When I was in elementary school, I went to school, looking forward more to having fights with my playmates than to studying. I came home from school with new scratches almost every day, but I was never scolded, unless I went [arrived] home crying.

(ii) When I was a primary school boy, it was not so much what I studied at school that amused me, as the scuffles I had with my playfellows. Nearly every day I used to go home with cuts and bruises, but as long as I didn't come home in tears, I was never reproved.

☆

第12章 教育・勉強・学校

───〈例題 5〉────────────
私は慎重な性質で，勉強もゆっくり，着実にする．学校でも，忍耐力を要求する学科が私にはとても面白かった．スポーツも同じで，短距離はだめだが，長距離は得意だった．大学で，古典を選択したのは，性質上，私に似合っていると思われたからだ．

■[語 句]「忍耐力を要求する学科」subjects which needed [demanded] perseverance /「短距離」sprinting, running fast (for a short distance) /「長距離」jogging long distances, long-distance running /「古典」classical literature

■[考え方]「勉強も，ゆっくり，着実にする」は，「ゆっくりと着実なやり方で，勉強する」と訳す．「...学科が私には面白かった」は，「私は...学科が楽しかった」と解し，enjoy を用いる．「スポーツも同じ」は，「スポーツということになっても，同じだ」と考える．when it comes to ～ の口語表現を用い，It was the same when it came to sports とするか，または，It was the same with sports とする．「古典を選択したのは，...私に似合っていると思われたからだ」は，「古典の研究に決めた，なぜならば，それが私によく似合っていると思われたからだ (I seemed well suited for it)」か，後半を，「それが私にとって理想的な学科だと思われたからだ」とする

〈 解　答　例 〉

(i) I am rather cautious by nature and work in a slow but steady way. At school I enjoyed subjects which demanded patience. It was the same when it came to sports; I was poor at running fast but good at jogging long distances. When I went to university, I decided to study classical literature because, by nature, I seemed well suited for it.

(**ii**) I am a cautious person. When I'm studying, I work in a slow but steady way. At school the subjects I enjoyed most were those which needed perseverance, and it was the same with sports; I was a good long-distance runner but I was a poor sprinter. In college I chose classical literature because, by nature, it seemed the ideal subject for me.

第13章
政治・経済・産業

Check & Check

□トムソン氏は45歳で政界に入った ⇨ Mr. Thompson entered [went into] politics at the age of 45.

□鈴木氏は次の選挙で，国会議員に立候補するらしい ⇨ It is likely that Mr. Suzuki will run for Diet in the next election.
　▶「国会議員に立候補する」は run for Diet 《日》[Congress 《米》], stand for Parliament 《英》という

□大統領は就任して間もなく暗殺された ⇨ The president was assassinated soon after he took office.
　▶take office は「(特に大統領，大臣などの公職などに)就任する」の意で，無冠詞．「辞任する」⇨ leave office

□君のお父さんは毎日何時に出勤しますか ⇨ What time does

your father go to the office every day?
▶「出勤する」は go to the office といい，定冠詞をつけて用いる．ただし，同義の go to work は無冠詞

□政党 ⇨ a political party
▶「与党」⇨ the Government Party, the ruling party /「与党の自民党」⇨ the ruling Liberal-Democratic Party /「野党」⇨ the Opposition Party

□国会は開会中です ⇨ The Diet is sitting.
▶「国会」は，しばしば大文字で始め，定冠詞を伴う．Congress《米》, Parliament《英》は，大文字で始め，無冠詞．「開会中」は be in session ともいう

□彼は政界の事情に通じている ⇨ He is familiar with political affairs.
▶「事情に通じている」の表現には，He is well informed about political affairs. も用いられる．「消息筋」⇨ well-informed sources

□アメリカ合衆国 ⇨ the United States of America
▶略して，the USA, または the States という．必ず，定冠詞 the をつける

□英国 ⇨ the United Kingdom (of Great Britain and Northern Ireland). 略して，the UK ともいう
▶「英連邦」⇨ the British Commonwealth of Nations. 略して，Great Britain, または Britain

□欧州連合 ⇨ the European Union. 略して，the EU. 定冠詞 the をつける
▶「拡大 EU」⇨ an expanded EU

□彼が駐米大使に任ぜられた ⇨ He has been appointed ambassador to the United States.
▶前置詞に注意．「大使館」⇨ an embassy

第13章　政治・経済・産業

☐外交官になる ⇨ go into the diplomatic service
▶「外交官」⇨ a diplomat

☐アフリカのその国は，最近中国と外交関係を樹立した ⇨ That African country has recently established diplomatic relations with China.
▶この relation は，通例複数形

☐日本は1956年に国連加盟を許可された ⇨ Japan gained [obtained] admission to the United Nations in 1956.
▶動詞表現：Japan was admitted to the United Nations in 1956.
▶「国連加盟国」⇨ a member nation of the United Nations

☐世界平和に貢献する ⇨ contribute to the peace of the world
▶the peace of the world を world peace ともいう

☐われらは今日，幸いに世界各国と和親の状態にある ⇨ We are fortunately at peace with all the world today.
▶「平和国家」⇨ a peace-loving nation

☐議案を提出する ⇨ introduce [submit] a bill

☐法案を可決[通過]する ⇨ adopt [pass, approve] a bill
▶「食事の勘定は私が払うよ」⇨ I'll pay the bill for the meal. この bill は「勘定書」の意

☐政府は抜本的なインフレ抑制策を講じるべきだ ⇨ The government should take [adopt] drastic measures to control inflation.
▶この measure は通例複数形．steps も同義

☐テッドの商売は繁盛している ⇨ Ted is doing (a) good business.
▶「繁盛する」は do (a) good business，または do a good

trade ともいう

□ますます多くの外国の会社が日本で商売をしている ⇨ More and more foreign companies are doing business in Japan.
　▶do business と類似の表現 (a), (b) に注意
　「私どもはあの商社と取り引きをしています」
　　(a) We have dealings with that trading firm.
　　(b) We carry on [have] transactions with that trading firm.
　dealing も transaction も通例複数形

□この店は羊毛品をあきなっている ⇨ This shop deals in woolen goods.
　▶「米の小売[卸し]商」⇨ a retail [wholesale] dealer in rice /「不動産売買業者」⇨ a real estate dealer

□舶来品より品質のよい国産品がたくさんある ⇨ There are many kinds of Japanese goods which are better in quality than foreign goods.
　▶「国産品」⇨ domestic goods, home-made articles /「舶来品」⇨ imported goods, foreign-made articles

□自動車工業は不況に見舞われている ⇨ The automobile industry is going through a recession.
　▶recession は無冠詞で用いるのが普通

□当市では諸物価が高い ⇨ Everything is expensive in this city.
　▶「物価が上[下]がっている」⇨ Prices are rising [declining].

□カナダの生活は，彼が思ったほど金がかからない ⇨ Living in Canada is not as expensive as he thought it would be.
　▶この文に動詞 cost を用いると，Living in Canada doesn't

第13章　政治・経済・産業

cost him as much as he thought it would. となる

☐国の経済状態を向上させる ⇨ improve the state of the economy

☐日本の経済事情 ⇨ Japan's economic affairs

☐今年は米が豊作です ⇨ We have a bumper rice crop this year.
　▶have a bumper crop は「豊作である」の意の熟語.「不作である」⇨ have a poor crop

☐この地方は，酪農に従事している農夫が多い ⇨ Many farmers are engaged in dairy farming in this area.

☐その会社は自動車の輸出で利益を得た ⇨ The company made profits from car exports.
　▶「利益を得る」は, make profits のほかに, earn, gain, get (profits) などが用いられる

☐その会社は先月倒産した ⇨ The company went into bankruptcy last month.
　▶形容詞表現：The company went bankrupt last month.

☐労働者は賃上げ要求してストに入った ⇨ The workers went on (a) strike, calling for higher wages.
　▶「ストをする」を口語で, walk out ともいう.「賃金」の wage は複数形が普通

☐費用を切り詰める ⇨ cut down expenses
　▶「出費を惜しまない」の意の熟語は, spare no expense という

☐この商品は供給より需要の方が多い ⇨ The demand for these goods exceeds the supply.
　▶「供給が需要に応じられない」⇨ The supply does not meet the demand.

□この品は売れ行きがよい ⇨ These articles are much in demand.

□国内生産だけではわれわれの需要をすべて満たすことはできない ⇨ Domestic production alone cannot satisfy all our demands.
　▶「需要を満たす」は，satisfy のほかに，[fill, meet, supply] all our demands なども用いられる

□私はいま就職口をさがしている ⇨ I am now looking [hunting] for a job.

□就職を申し込む ⇨ apply for a position

□うちの娘は速記者の職についた ⇨ Our daughter got [took] a job as a stenographer [shorthand typist].
　▶「その貿易会社に就職する」⇨ get a job with the trading firm（前置詞 with に注意）

□ボブは病気のため失職した ⇨ Bob lost his job because of illness.
　▶「失業している」⇨ be out of employment [work, (a) job]
　▶「リストラにあう」⇨ be fired [laid off]

□失業対策 ⇨ a relief measure for the unemployed

□両国間に貿易摩擦が生じる ⇨ cause trade friction between the two countries
　▶trade imbalance（不均衡）ともいう

□その事業は多大の資本金を要する ⇨ The enterprise requires a lot of capital.

□私たちはその事業に多額の資金をつぎ込んだ ⇨ We have invested a lot of capital in that business.
　▶capital の代わりに，money も使う

第13章 政治・経済・産業

- □難民救済の資金を調達する ⇒ raise funds for the relief of the refugees
  - ▶「慈善の目的で募金する」⇒ raise money for charity
- □暮らし向きがよい[悪い] ⇒ be well [badly] off
- □まさかの時に備え貯蓄する ⇒ save up for a rainy day
  - ▶for a rainy day は,「困窮, 零落(れいらく)の時」の意
- □家事を手伝う亭主が多くなっている ⇒ More and more husbands are ready to help with the housework.
  - ▶「家事をする」⇒ do the housework. この表現は, 通例定冠詞をつける
- □年功序列制と終身雇用 ⇒ the seniority system and lifetime employment
- □父は健康がすぐれないという理由で辞職した ⇒ My father has resigned on the grounds of ill health.
  - ▶「辞表を提出する」⇒ hand in one's resignation
- □叔父は2年前現役を退き, 今は年金で暮らしている ⇒ My uncle retired from active service two years ago and now lives on a pension.

Let's Try

【Ⅰ】下の囲みの中に与えられている名詞を, 英文の空所に入れ, 日本文の意味になるように完成しなさい.

1. The Government began to ease (　　) on imports.
  (政府は輸入規制をゆるめ始めた)
2. The Government should take effective (　　) to promote domestic industry.
  (政府は国内産業を促進すべき有効な方策を講じるべきだ)

3. Parliament will not be in (　　) again until after Christmas.
　　(議会はクリスマス後まで再び開会しない)
4. He left (　　) because he disagreed with the prime minister.
　　(彼は首相と意見が合わず辞任した)
5. He did not enter (　　) until he was forty-five.
　　(彼は45歳までは政界にはいらなかった)
6. Buying on (　　) often means throwing your money away.
　　(衝動買いは銭失いだ)
7. His company is having a hard (　　).
　　(彼の会社は不景気だ)
8. There was a good apple (　　) this year, so they should be cheap.
　　(今年はリンゴがたくさんなったので，安くなりそうだ)

```
office      service     time      recession    politics
restrictions      crop      impulse       session
measures      government
```

■[ヒント]　1.「制限」　2.「対策」　3.「開会中」　4.「公職」無冠詞.　5.「政治」　6.「衝動」　7. recession は無冠詞.　8.「収穫」. a good (　　) of apples ともいう

■[解答]　1. restrictions　2. measures　3. session　4. office　5. politics　6. impulse　7. time　8. crop

【II】下の囲みの中に与えられている動詞を，必要に応じて変化させ，英文の空所に入れ，日本文の意味になるようにしなさい．

1. It cannot be said that democracy has completely

第13章　政治・経済・産業

(　　) root in our country.
(民主主義が我が国に完全に根づいているとは言えない)
2. The Diet (　　) of the House of Representatives and the House of Councilors.
(国会は衆議院と参議院とから成っている)
3. The company is (　　) well.
(あの会社は景気がいい)
4. Since the big supermarket moved into the neighborhood, the local retailers have (　　) a lot of customers.
(大きなスーパーマーケットが進出して，この辺の小売店は客を食われている)
5. Progress in industry (　　) life easier, but at the same time it produces numerous harmful side effects.
(産業の発達によって生活が便利になっているが同時に，数多くの弊害も出てきている)
6. Advertisements often (　　) you to buy more things than you need.
(広告のため，必要ないものまで買うことがある)

---
do　　cause　　lose　　make　　grow　　consist
take　　let

■[ヒント]　1. strike root ともいう．現在完了形．　2.「成っている」は受身で，be made up of ともいう．　3. do a good business と同義．進行形．　4.「失ってしまった」と解す．現在完了形．　5. S+V+O+C の文型．　6. S+V+O+C の文型.
■[解答]　1. taken　2. consists　3. doing　4. lost　5. makes　6. cause

Let's Memorize

1. イギリスの国会は上院と下院とからなる.

    Parliament is made up of the House of Lords and the House of Commons.

2. わが国はもっと国民の福祉の向上につとめるべきだ.

    Our country should try more to improve the welfare of the people.

3. 彼は激しく政府の対米貿易政策を批難した.

    He bitterly criticized the government's trade policy toward the U.S.

4. 政府は公共事業におおいに力を入れている.

    The government is putting a great deal of effort into public works.

5. 首相は来年8月にモスクワを訪問し, ロシア首脳とトップ会談を行なう.

    The Prime Minister will go to Moscow in August next year for a summit meeting with Russian leaders.

6. この頃の学生は, 概して, 政治に対する関心がうすい.

    Generally, students these days have little interest in politics.

7. そのデパートは横浜へ進出しようと計画している.

    The department store is planning to open a branch in Yokohama.

8. あの店はいいお得意さんをたくさんもっている.

    That store has a lot of good customers.

9. あの会社は経営がうまくいっている.

    Business at that company is going well.

10. 会社が倒産して以来，彼は生活に苦しんでいる．	He has had a hard life since the company went bankrupt.
11. 東京は，生活費が高くつく．	Tokyo is an expensive city to live in.
12. 日本車は海外で人気を博している．	Japanese cars enjoy great popularity overseas.
13. オーストラリア政府は，日本に果物と肉の輸入制限を緩和するよう求めている．	The Australian government is urging Japan to ease restrictions on imports of fruit and meat.
14. 航空機を生産するためには高度な技術力が必要とされる．	Manufacturing airplanes calls for a high level of technology.
15. 日本が高度な工業国であるというのは，常識である．	Everyone knows that Japan is a highly industrialized country.

Exercises

〈例題 1〉

　国際貿易に依存するわが国の経済にとって，貿易摩擦問題を解消できるか否かは死活の問題である．なんとしても解決の方策を見つけねばならない．

■[語 句]　「国際貿易」foreign trade, international trade /「依存する」depend on /「貿易摩擦問題」the trade friction problem /「死活の問題」a question of life or death, a matter of vital importance /「なんとしても」at all cost(s), by any means possible

■[考え方]　「国際貿易に依存するわが国の経済にとって」は，

「わが国の経済は国際貿易に依存しているので」と解す．「〜解消できるか否かは」は「〜の解決は」とすれば十分．「なんとしても解決の方策を見つけねばならない」は，「どんな手段でも，この問題を解決する方法を見つけねばならぬ」と解し，受動態でも，能動態でもよい．

〈解　答　例〉

(i) Because the economy of our country depends on foreign trade, the settlement of the trade friction problem is a question of life or death. A way of working out this problem should be found at all costs.

(ii) Resolving the trade friction problem is a matter of vital importance because our country is dependent on international trade. We must, by any means possible, find a way to solve this problem.

☆

―――〈例題 2〉―――
現在の世界経済は1930年代以来最も重大な危機に直面している．できるだけ早く，有効な措置が講じられなければ，南北間の格差は一段と広がり，国際的な政治・経済秩序が崩壊することも考えられる．

■[語句]　「現代の世界経済」the present-day economy /「〜に直面している」be faced with 〜 /「有効な措置が講じられる」effective measures are taken /「南北間の格差」the gaps between the North and the South, the North-South gaps /「政治・経済秩序」political and economic order

■[考え方]　第一文の，「〜に直面している」に動詞 face か confront を用いる．「有効な措置が講じられなければ」は If some effective measures are not taken, または Unless the proper steps are taken と訳す．「格差は一段と広がり，国際的

な政治・経済秩序が崩壊することも考えられる」は,「格差がさらに大きくなり, 世界の政治と経済の秩序が崩壊するであろう」と未来時制を用いる

〈 解 答 例 〉

(i) The present-day world economy is faced with the most serious crisis since the nineteen-thirties. If some effective measures are not taken as soon as possible, the gaps between the North and the South will become much larger, and the political and economic order of the world will break down.

(ii) The gravest crisis since the 1930's is confronting the economy of the world. Unless the proper steps are taken as rapidly as possible, the North-South gaps will get wider, resulting in a possible collapse of international political and economic order.

☆

―〈例題 3〉―
　過去数年, 日本車の欧州への輸出は増え続けており, 大きな経済問題のひとつになっている. こうした問題を円満に解決するために, 関係する各国政府は率直に話し合う必要がある.

■[語 句] 「日本車」Japanese cars /「大きな経済問題」a major economic problem
■[考え方] 「日本車の欧州への輸出は増え続けており...」は現在完了時制を用い,「欧州へ輸出されている日本車の数が, 着実に増加している」か,「日本が欧州に輸出している車の数が堅実に増加している」と解す.「増加」を名詞形にし, There has been a steady increase in the number of Japanese cars being exported to Europe. または,「増加する」と動詞表現で

Japan has steadily increased the number of cars she exports to Europe. とする.「こうした問題を円満に解決するために」は, in order to bring this problem to an amicable settlement, または, in order to work out a satisfactory solution to this problem とする.「率直に話し合う必要がある」は, it is necessary...to の構文を用い, it is necessary...to consult openly and honestly with each other とする. または, ...should talk frankly with each other など, いずれでもよい.「関係する各国政府は...」(the governments of the countries concerned ...) の位置はどこがよいか考えてみよう.

〈解　答　例〉

(i) For the last several years there has been a steady increase in the number of Japanese cars being exported to Europe; this is a major economic problem.　In order to bring this problem to an amicable settlement, it is necessary for the governments of the countries concerned to consult openly and honestly with each other.

(ii) Every year, for the past few years, Japan has steadily increased the number of cars she exports to Europe.　This has become one of the major economic problems between the two.　In order to work out a satisfactory solution to this problem, the governments of the countries concerned should talk frankly with each other.

☆

第13章　政治・経済・産業

──〈例題 4〉──
　もし石油がなかったとしたら，20世紀の歴史はまったく違ったものになっていたであろう．現代文明の象徴である自動車や飛行機は存在しなかったろう．また，電気のようなエネルギーを現在のように安価で豊富に入手できるかということも疑問である．

■[語句]　「20世紀の歴史」twentieth-century history, the history of the 20th century /「現代文明の象徴」the symbols of present-day civilization /「安価で豊富に」at a low price or in abundance, cheaply and abundantly /「疑問である」it is doubtful whether 〜

■[考え方]　「もし石油がなかったとしたら...違ったものになっていたであろう」は，If there were no petroleum, twentieth-century history would be quite different... と仮定法過去を用いる．「自動車や飛行機は存在しなかったろう」は，If 節が省略され，過去形の助動詞で帰結節を作る．「存在しなかったろう」は「発明されなかったろう」と解し，would probably not have been invented とすることもできる．「...も疑問である」には，there is little doubt that 〜 を用いると，that 節の中に，「石油がなければ，電気のようなエネルギーは...入手できないことは，疑いない」とする．また，it is doubtful whether 〜 を用いれば，whether 節は，「石油がなければ，電気のようなエネルギーが...入手されることは疑わしい」と訳す．両者とも，that 及び whether 節の中は，仮定法過去形を用いる．

〈解　答　例〉

(i)　If there were no petroleum, twentieth-century history would be entirely different. The automobile and the plane, which are symbols of present-day civilization, could hardly exist. Moreover, there is little doubt that

政治・経済・産業

without petroleum, electrical energy could not be produced at such a low price or in such abundance as it is today.

(ii) But for oil, the history of the 20th century would be quite different from what it is. Cars or aeroplanes, the symbols of modern-day civilization, would probably not have been invented. Besides, it is also doubtful whether, without petroleum, energy like electricity could be obtained as cheaply and as abundantly as it is today.

☆

―――〈例題 5〉―――
　かつては"機械は考えうるか"という問いは，意味をなさないと考えられた．しかし，最近の工学の発展はめざましく，たとえば，チェスをする機械をも作り上げている．さらに，ひとりで思考できる機械さえ考案されたといわれている．しかし，問題は，真の意味における，自ら考えることができる機械を作る可能性があるか，ということである．

■[語 句]　「意味をなす」make sense /「工学の発展」progress in electronics /「さらに」moreover, what is more /「真の意味における」in the true sense of the word

■[考え方]　第一文の，「"機械は考えうるか"という問いは意味をなさないと考えられた」は，It was once thought that ... を用い，「...という問い」は，次の2通りに訳す．すなわち，the question, "Can machines think?" か，the question of whether machines can think とする．「最近の工学の発展はめざましく，チェスをする機械をも作り上げている」は，「最近のめざましい工学の発展のため，チェスのできる機械を作り上げることが可能となっている」と解し，現在完了を用いる．「ひとりで思考できる機械」は a machine which can think for itself

第13章 政治・経済・産業

とするか,「筋の通った思考のできる機械」と解し, a machine which can think logically とすることもよい。最後の,「真の意味における,自ら考えることができる機械を作る可能性があるか」を,「人間と同じように思考できる機械を作ることが可能かどうか」と直す。

〈解 答 例〉

(i) It was once thought that the question, " Can machines think? " didn't make sense. However, because of recent amazing progress in electronics, it has been possible to invent, for example, a machine which can play chess. What is more, it is said that even a machine which can think for itself has been devised. The problem is: Is there any possibility of inventing a machine which can think for itself in the true sense of the word?

(ii) The question of whether machines can think was once thought to make no sense. But recent remarkable developments in electronics have made it possible to make, for example, a machine which can play chess. Moreover, they say that a machine which can think logically has been invented. The important question is, however, whether it is possible to make a machine which can think in the same way as humans do.

第14章
道徳・思想・感情

Check & Check

□ 彼は正しいと信じることを言う勇気がある ⇨ He has the courage to say what he believes (to be) right.
　▶courage には必ず定冠詞 the をつける．形容詞表現：He is courageous enough to say what he believes right.

□ 山田氏は責任感が強い ⇨ Mr. Yamada has a strong sense of responsibility.

□ この仕事は私が責任をもって明日までに終えます ⇨ I will take [assume] the responsibility of finishing this work by tomorrow.

□ その子供は善悪を区別するくらいの分別はある ⇨ That child has the sense to be able to tell good from evil.

□私は他人の陰口を言うほど無分別ではない ⇒ I know better than to speak ill of others behind their backs.
　▶同意表現：I have more sense than to speak ill of others behind their backs.

□彼は清廉潔白な人だという評判です ⇒ He has the reputation of being a man of integrity.

□彼女のいい所は，愛嬌(あいきょう)があるということだ ⇒ A good thing about her is that she is charming.
　▶「彼の悪い所は，怒りやすいことだ」⇒ A bad thing about him is that he loses his temper easily.

□彼がどんな性格の人か知らない ⇒ I don't know what kind of (a) person he is.
　▶同意表現：I don't know what he is like.《注》I don't know what kind of person he is *like*. は誤り

□個性を知る1つの方法は，その人の趣味を知ることである ⇒ One of the ways of knowing a person's personality is to know his [her] hobbies.
　▶personality は，「個性，殊に他人に映じる容貌，動作などを含めた人柄」，character は，「道徳的な意味での性格」をいう

□父は行儀作法のやかましい人だった ⇒ My father was very particular about (good) manners.
　▶この manner は，複数形

□彼は礼儀正しい ⇒ He has good manners.
　▶同意表現：He is well-mannered.

□彼女は礼儀を知らない ⇒ She has [knows] no manners.
　▶同意表現：She is ill-mannered.

□次郎のような行儀の悪い子を私は見たことがない ⇒ Jiro is

the worst-behaved child I have ever seen.
　▶同意表現: I have never seen a boy who behaves so badly as Jiro.

□子供の頃, 彼女は親にとても従順だった ⇨ When she was a small child, she showed great obedience to her parents.
　▶形容詞表現: When she was a small child, she was very obedient to her parents.

□彼は身の振り方について私の忠告に従った ⇨ He took [followed] my advice as to what he should do.
　▶「忠告に従う」を obey one's advice と言うのは誤り. obey は, 目的語として, 「法律や人間」などを従える

□父は根気と勤勉で, 財産を築いた ⇨ My father has made a fortune by means of perseverance and industry.
　▶fortune が, 「財産」の意のときは, 不定冠詞 a をつける

□彼は運良く, 大学入試に 1 度で合格した ⇨ He had the good fortune to pass the college entrance examination at his first attempt.
　▶形容詞表現: He was fortunate enough to pass the college entrance examination at his first attempt.

□祖母はいまだに外国人に対して偏見を持っている ⇨ My grandmother still has a prejudice against foreign people.
　▶形容詞表現: My grandmother is still prejudiced against foreign people.

□彼は信頼できる. 徳の高い人だから. ⇨ You can trust him; he is a man of high virtue.

□エリザの勇敢さにはいつも感心する ⇨ I always have [feel]

admiration for Eliza's bravery.
　▶動詞表現：I admire Eliza for her bravery.

□われわれは両親に，われわれのためにしてくれたすべてのことに対して感謝すべきである ⇒ We should be grateful to our parents for all they have done for us.
　▶grateful は「人間」に，thankful は「神の摂理」に，「感謝する」意．be grateful to a person for something の前置詞 for に注意

□われわれは，田村夫人の誠意ある援助に対し，謝意を表した ⇒ We have expressed our thanks to Mrs. Tamura for her cordial assistance.
　▶この表現では，thank は複数形．動詞表現：We have thanked Mrs. Tamura for her cordial assistance.
　▶express one's thanks to ～ for... の thanks の代わりに，gratitude も用いられる

□君は試験に合格するよう，真剣に努力すべきだ ⇒ You should make a serious effort to pass the examination.
　▶「努力する」は make an effort と単数形でも，make efforts と複数形でもよい

□約束したら，守るべきだ ⇒ If you make a promise, you should keep it.
　▶「約束を守る[破る]」は，keep [break] one's promise, または，keep [break] one's word という

□入試に失敗したからといって，気を落とすな ⇒ Don't become discouraged, just because you failed the entrance examination.
　▶「落胆する」は be discouraged, be disheartened, be disappointed なども用いられる．いずれも受動態に注意

□目的達成のためには，あらゆる困難に打ち勝たねばならぬ ⇒

You should overcome all difficulties in order to accomplish your object.
　▶「困難に打ち勝つ」は overcome [conquer] difficulties と, 複数形が通例.「彼は財政困難に陥っている」⇨ He is having financial difficulties. この表現も, しばしば複数形

□一週間中, ツイていた ⇨ I have had good luck all week.
　▶have good luck は「運がいい」の意の熟語. luck は無冠詞. 形容詞表現: I have been lucky all week.
　▶「運が悪い」は have no [bad] luck

□彼は私の新調の洋服をほめてくれた ⇨ He paid me a compliment on my new dress.
　▶動詞表現: He complimented me on my new dress.

□吉田先生は, すべての生徒に深い愛情を抱いていた ⇨ Miss Yoshida felt [had] deep affection for all her students.

□息子を車の事故で亡くしたアリスに同情しています ⇨ I feel [have] sympathy for Alice who lost her son in a car accident.
　▶この sympathy は通例無冠詞. feel sympathy for ～ の動詞表現は sympathize with, 形容詞表現は be sympathetic toward

□彼女は事故で自分の子を殺した運転手を憎んでいる ⇨ She feels [has] a hatred for [of] the driver who killed her child in an accident.
　▶この表現では, hatred に不定冠詞 a をつける. feel a hatred for ～ は, 動詞表現では hate ～ となる

□私は試験の結果に満足した ⇨ I found satisfaction in the results of the examination.
　▶動詞表現: I was satisfied with the results of the examination.

□彼は休みに，ひとりで方々を旅するのを楽しみにしています ⇨ He finds [takes] pleasure in going places alone on his day off.
　▶「楽しみにしている」の表現は，find pleasure in のほかに，find delight [enjoyment, entertainment, joy] in などがある

□彼は他人の気持ちに対して思いやりがない ⇨ He has no consideration for the feelings of other people.

□園遊会を計画するときは，天候を考慮に入れねばならない ⇨ When you're planning a garden party, you'll have to take the weather into account.
　▶「~を考慮に入れる」の熟語は，take ~ into account [consideration], consider ~ seriously, make allowance for ~ などがある

□彼は他人の苦しみに全く無とんちゃくだった ⇨ He showed complete indifference to the sufferings of other people.
　▶形容詞表現：He was completely indifferent to the sufferings of other people.

□ジェインは家事をうまく切り盛りする能力を自慢している ⇨ Jane takes pride in her ability to keep house well.
　▶pride は無冠詞．動詞表現：Jane prides herself on her ability to keep house well. 形容詞表現：Jane is proud of her ability to keep house well.

□人は年をとるにつれ，人生のはかなさを思案し始める ⇨ As you get older, you begin to reflect on how uncertain life is.
　▶「人生のはかなさ」を the uncertainty of life ともいえる

□お邪魔してすみませんが，ちょっとお話ししたいのですが ⇨ I'm sorry to disturb you, but could I speak to you for a moment?

▶sorry+to 原形不定詞は，現在または未来に起こる行為に対し陳謝を表わす

□昨夜，たいへん遅くお電話して本当に申し訳ありません ⇨ I'm really sorry to have called you up very late last night.
▶sorry+to have+過去分詞は，過去に起こった行為に対し，陳謝を表わす．同意表現：I'm sorry for calling you up [having called you up] very late last night.

□スーザンは高校時代，もっと勉強しなかったことを後悔している ⇨ Susan feels regret for not having worked harder when she was in high school.
▶動詞表現：Susan regrets not having worked harder when she was in high school. [Susan regrets that she didn't work harder...]

□あなたは自分の不作法を彼女におわびしなさい ⇨ You must make an apology to her for your rudeness.
▶動詞表現：You must apologize to her for your rudeness. 名詞表現は堅苦しいので，口語では動詞表現が使われることが多い．apologize は自動詞

□その不良少年は行ないを改めると約束した ⇨ The bad boy promised to mend his ways.
▶mend one's ways は，「行状を改める」の意の熟語．way は複数形であることに注意

□母の誕生日に何を買っていいか見当もつかない ⇨ I have no idea (of) what to buy for my mother for her birthday.
▶have no idea (of)+疑問節は，「～がわからない」の意の熟語．not have any idea, not have the slightest [faintest, foggiest] idea ともいう

□いい考えを思いついた ⇨ I hit on a good idea.

▶「考え」を主語にし、A good idea struck [occurred to] me. ともいう

□早合点する ⇨ jump [leap, rush] to conclusions
▶that 節を従えるときは、jump to the conclusion that ～ と定冠詞 the を伴う

□顔に冷たい水をかけたら、彼は正気づいた ⇨ He came to his senses when we threw cold water on his face.
▶come to one's senses は、「意識を回復する」の意の熟語. sense は複数形になることに注意

□妻はそのアパートを見るやいなや、気に入った ⇨ My wife took a fancy to the apartment house as soon as she saw it.
▶「気に入る」は take a fancy *to*, take a liking *to* という. 「好きである」は、have a fancy *for*, have a liking *for* という. これらの表現では、不定冠詞をつける

□藤原氏は戦時中、無抵抗主義に固執した ⇨ Mr. Fujiwara stuck to [lived up to] his principles of non-resistance during the war.
▶「～の主義を貫く」の意の熟語は、stick to one's principles of ～ といい、複数形

□彼は外科医として前途有望だ ⇨ He has a bright future (before him) as a surgeon.
▶この表現では、future に不定冠詞と形容詞をつける. 「前途が暗い」は、have a dark future という

□いつも自分の言い分ばかり押し通そうとするのは愚かだ ⇨ It is silly of you to insist on getting your own way all the time.
▶get [have] one's own way は「思い通りにする、我を押し通す」の意の熟語

□日本の学生は愛校精神が強い者が多い ⇨ Many students in Japan have great school spirit.
　▶この表現では，spirit は無冠詞で単数形,「忠誠心」の意.「愛社精神」⇨ company spirit

□公共心のある ⇨ public-spirited

□公衆道徳に欠ける ⇨ be lacking in public morality [morals]

□理想を実現する ⇨ realize [achieve] one's ideal

□母はその吉報を聞いて，狂喜した ⇨ My mother was beside herself with joy when she heard the good news.
　▶be beside oneself は,「(歓喜や悲しみのため)われを忘れている」の意の熟語

□スリにご用心 ⇨ Be on your guard against pickpockets.
　▶be on one's guard は「用心する」意の熟語.「油断する」⇨ be off one's guard

□何の目的で，そんなに懸命に仕事をしているのだ ⇨ What is your aim in working so hard?
　▶口語では，What are you working so hard for? ともいう

Let's Try

【Ⅰ】 日本文に相当するように，英文の空所に下の囲みの中に与えられている語を適当に変化させて入れなさい.
1. 私は考えをまとめるのに少し時間がいる.
　　I need some time to (　　) my thoughts.
2. この仕事は経験がものを言う.
　　It's experience that (　　) in this job.
3. この仕事をちょっと手伝ってください.
　　Would you please (　　) me a hand with this work?

第14章 道徳・思想・感情

4. 物事は理論どおりには運ばないものだ.
   Things never (　　) out according to theory.
5. ちょっとお願いがあるんですけど.
   Excuse me, but could you (　　) me a favor?

---
count　　help　　organize　　pay　　lend　　work
do　　ask

■[ヒント] 1.「組織する」という意味でよく使われる他動詞. 2.「価値をもつ」の意の自動詞. 3. (　　) me a hand=help me. 4. (　　) out=have a good result. 5.「お願いがある」は, Could you (　　) me a favor?=May I ask a favor of you? となる
■[解答] 1. organize　2. counts　3. lend　4. work　5. do

【II】 下の語句を適当に配列して, つぎの日本文の英訳となるようにしなさい.
1. 年をとるにつれて, 人は一般に頑固になる.
   they grow, become, as, people generally, older, stubborn
2. 彼の考え方は私のと似ている.
   mine, of thinking, very, similar, his way, to, is
3. 私にはその気の毒な娘を慰めることしかできない.
   the poor girl, I can, is, console, all, do, try to
4. 彼はこうと決めたら最後, 人の言うことなど聞かない.
   what, his mind, has to, once, he won't listen to, he has, made up, say, anyone else

■[ヒント] 1. 接続詞 as は, 比較級を伴い,「～につれて」の意. 2.「私の(考え方)」は, mine とする. 3. All=The only thing と解する. (to) try の前は to が省略できる. 4.「こうと決めたら最後」は,「いったん決めたら」とし, once を接続詞にする.「人の言うこと」は「他人が言いたいこと」と考える.

■ [解答] 1. People generally become stubborn as they grow older. 2. His way of thinking is very similar to mine. 3. All I can do is try to console the poor girl. 4. Once he has made up his mind, he won't listen to what anyone else has to say.

Let's Memorize

1. 人間の値打ちは，その人の行為によって決まる．

   A man's worth is determined by what he does.

2. 善行はたいてい報われるものだ．

   People are generally rewarded for their good deeds.

3. 良心に従って行動しなさい．

   Act in accordance with your conscience.

4. その計画は実行に移される前に中止された．

   The plan was canceled before it was put into action.

5. 君が何を言いたいのか，さっぱり分からない．

   I don't have the slightest idea what you're trying to say.

6. 彼の言っていることは筋が通っている．

   What he says makes sense.

7. 昨夜のパーティーで，私にあんな失礼なことを言って恥ずかしくないのか．

   You should be ashamed of yourself for saying such a rude thing to me at the party last night.

8. どうもこの頃の君の態度はおかしい．

   There's something strange about your attitude these days.

9. 彼女のちょっとした思い

   I'm always impressed by

第14章 道徳・思想・感情

やりにはいつも感心する．

her little kindnesses.

10. 彼は私の気持ちを傷つけても，何にもなかったようにふるまっている．

He hurts my feelings and now acts as if nothing had happened.

11. 彼女は他人の評価を気にしない．

She's indifferent to what others think of her.

12. 彼に無礼な態度をとったことを心から詫びた．

I apologized sincerely for having acted rudely to him.

13. それは願ってもないことだ．

You could ask for nothing better.

14. 私の感謝の気持ちは言葉ではとても言い尽くせません．

It's impossible for me to express my gratitude in words.

15. 彼はどんな困難にあっても，落胆しない．

He doesn't lose heart in the face of any difficulty.

Exercises

〈例題 1〉

われわれは自分自身の行動を，だいたい律している．何かを食べたいと思えば食べ，食べたくないと思えば食べない．常に自分の意志に従い，自分の感ずるままに，行動している．

■[語 句] 「行動を律する」have control over one's own actions, control one's own behavior /「だいたい」for the most part, generally speaking /「自分の意志に従い」(act) of one's own accord, of one's own free will /「行動する」take action, act

■[考え方] 「われわれは自分自身の行動を律している」は

「われわれは自分自身の行動を完全に支配している」とか,「われわれは自分自身のふるまいを支配する能力をもっている」と訳す. 第2文の,「何かを食べたいと思えば食べ」は, When we feel like eating something, we eat it と直し, eat を他動詞として扱う. また, 同じ文に自動詞の eat を用いて, We eat when we want to. としてもよい. 第3文の「自分の感ずるままに」は,「われわれが感ずるままに従って」とか,「われわれがいちばん良いと感ずるように」と解し, according to the way we feel か, in the way we feel best などと工夫する

〈解 答 例〉

(i) For the most part we have complete control over our own actions. When we feel like eating something, we eat it; we don't eat anything when we don't want to. We always take action of our own accord and according to the way we feel.

(ii) Generally speaking, we have the ability to control our own behavior. We eat when we want to, and don't eat when we don't want to. We are always acting of our own free will and in the way we feel best.

☆

―〈例題 2〉―
どういう訳か, 日本人は自分より年若い人の下で働くのをいやがります. 彼がどんなに優秀な人であっても, 自分より若ければ耐えられないのです.

■[語 句]「どういう訳か」for some reason or other, somehow /「優秀な」capable, competent /「耐えられる」put up with, stand

■[考え方]「自分より年若い人の下で働くのをいやがる」は,「自分たちより若い上司 (a boss) の下で働くのが嫌い」とする.

第14章　道徳・思想・感情

「彼がどんなに優秀な人であっても」は However [No matter how]＋形容詞＋主語＋動詞の譲歩構文を用いる．「優秀な」には excellent は不適当である

〈解　答　例〉

(i) For some reason or other, Japanese people hate to work under a person younger than themselves. If their boss is younger than they are, they cannot put up with him, no matter how capable he is.

(ii) Somehow, Japanese people are reluctant to work under the direction of a boss junior to them. No matter how competent he is, they can't stand it if he is younger.

☆

―〈例題 3〉――
　日本人とイギリス人は似ているところもありますが，全く似ていないところもあります．いちばん違うところは，私が思うに，日本人はどんなものも，新しければ新しいほどよいと考えるのに対して，イギリス人は古いほど価値があると思うことでしょう．

■[語　句]　「私が思うに」to my way of thinking
■[考え方]　「日本人とイギリス人は似ているところもあり，全く似ていないところもある」は，「日本人とイギリス人は，ある点では似ており，またある点では異なっている」と考え，「ある点では...またある点では」には in some ways..., but...in other ways の相関語句を用いる．「いちばん違うところは」は，「両国民の間にある最大の相違点」と解して主語にし，the greatest difference between the two peoples is... とする．「私が思うに」は，it seems to me, を文中に挿入する．「日本人は，どんなものも，新しければ新しいほどよいと考える」は，the＋比較級＋主語＋動詞, the＋比較級＋主語＋動詞 の比較構

文を用い,「どんなものも」は訳さなくてよい. 第2文の「日本人とイギリス人」は, the Japanese と the British の代わりに「前者」「後者」と考え the former, the latter (複数扱い) で表現する

〈解　答　例〉

(i) In some ways the Japanese and the British are very similar, but in other ways they are quite different. The greatest difference, it seems to me, between the two peoples is that the Japanese think that the newer something is, the better it is, while the British think that the older a thing is, the more valuable it is.

(ii) The Japanese and the British are similar in some respects, but quite different in others. The most remarkable difference between the two nations is, to my way of thinking, that the former think the newer the better, no matter what it is, while the latter think that a thing gets more valuable as it becomes older.

☆

────〈例題 4〉────
　われわれ日本人は自分が所属している集団から独立していると考えたり, 他人と全くかけ離れた行動をとることが苦手である. われわれがどのように行動するかは, 他人からどう思われるかによって影響されることが多い.

■[語　句]　「集団から独立している」independent of the group /「他人とかけ離れた行動をとる」act differently from others /「影響する」affect, have an influence on
■[考え方]　この文全体を一般論とすれば, the Japanese を用い, その代名詞として they を用いる. 他方,「われわれ日本人」を We Japanese と訳せば, 代名詞は we となる. 第1文の,

「われわれ日本人は...と考えたり,他人と全くかけ離れた行動をとることが苦手である」は,It is difficult for the Japanese to think..., or to act ~ の不定詞構文を用いる.また,difficult を名詞形にして,We have difficulty in ~ing の動名詞構文にする.「自分が所属している集団から独立していると考える」を直訳すると,think of themselves as being independent of the group to which they belong となる.これは,「自分の集団から分離して考える」と解し,associate oneself with ~ (~と共同する)の反意語を用いて dissociate ourselves from our own group とすることも可能.「われわれがどのように行動するかは,他人からどう思われるかによって,影響されることが多い」は,the way we behave, what we do, または our behavior などを主語とし,affect を受動態にする.「多い」は often と訳せばよい

〈 解　答　例 〉

(i)　It is difficult for the Japanese either to think of themselves as being independent of the group to which they belong, or to act quite differently from others. The way they behave is often affected by what others think of them.

(ii)　We Japanese have difficulty in dissociating ourselves from our own group or in taking action entirely different from other people. What others think of us often has a great influence on what we do.

第15章
社会・環境・国際事情

Check & Check

□現代社会において ⇨ in present-day society
　▶society は「(共通の文化・伝統・制度と利害をもつ集団的生活としての)社会」の意

□社会全体の福祉を増進する ⇨ promote the welfare of the whole community
　▶community は,「(個人に対する市町村,国家などの)共同体,地域社会」の意

□自分の住む社会の風習に従おうと努める者が多い ⇨ Many people try to conform to the ways of the community in which they live.

□よい社会人となる ⇨ become a respectable member of society

第15章　社会・環境・国際事情　　227

☐この国では20歳以上の者すべてに投票権がある ⇨ In this country everyone over 20 years of age has the right to vote.
　▶「投票権がある」は have the right to vote または have the right of voting という

☐法律はわれわれの権利を保護するためのもので，われわれの自由を奪うために作られたのではない ⇨ Laws are made to protect our rights and not to take away our liberty.

☐自衛権を行使する ⇨ exercise the right of self-defense
　▶この動詞 exercise は，use の意

☐基本的人権 ⇨ fundamental human rights

☐他人の権利を尊重する ⇨ respect the rights of others

☐言論[出版]の自由 ⇨ freedom of speech [the press]

☐アメリカの奴隷は1863年に解放された ⇨ The slaves in the United States gained their freedom in 1863.
　▶「解放される」は gain [be given] one's freedom という

☐会員はだれでも，自由に自分の見解を述べられる ⇨ Each member is at liberty to express his own views.
　▶be at liberty to ~ は be free to ~ と同義. liberty は「選択，意志の自由」を意味し，freedom は「他からの束縛を受けないことの自由」を暗示する

☐環境汚染についての君のご意見を聞かせてください ⇨ Let me have your opinion on environmental pollution.
　▶have one's opinion on ~ は「~について意見をもつ」の意の熟語

☐われわれは和夫君の統率力を高く買っている ⇨ We have a good [high] opinion of Kazuo's leadership ability.
　▶have a good [high] opinion of ~ は「~を高く評価して

いる」の意の熟語.「～を低く見る」は have a bad [low] opinion of ～ とする

☐世論は一般に政府の物価諸政策に賛成だった ⇨ Public opinion was largely in favor of the Government price policies.

☐現代の世界において,文化をはかる最も単純な尺度はなんですか ⇨ What is the simplest measure of culture in the modern world?

☐周囲を見回し,自由と寛容がいたるところに見られるならば,その社会の文化の水準は高いといえよう ⇨ If we look around us and find that liberality and tolerance are everywhere apparent, we may safely say that the standard of culture in that particular society is high.

☐ローナは2人の子供を産んだ ⇨ Lorna brought two children into the world.
　▶bring ～ into the world は「～(赤ん坊)を産む」の意の熟語. give birth to ～ も同義. come into the world [be born] は「生まれる」の意の熟語

☐実社会に出ると,サラリーマンになるという意味が分かるよ ⇨ You will realize what it means to be an office worker when you go out into the world.
　▶go out into the world は「実社会に出る」の意の熟語

☐立身出世する ⇨ rise in the world, get on in the world

☐彼は自由と人道のために,いろいろ尽くしてくれた ⇨ He has done [rendered, performed] many services to the cause of freedom and humanity.
　▶service は「尽力,奉仕」の意では,通例複数形

☐あなたのお役に立つならば,よろこんで援助いたしましょ

第15章　社会・環境・国際事情

う ⇨ I shall be only too pleased to help, if I can be of service to you.
　▶of service to＋人は「～の役に立つ」の意の熟語. of service は, useful, helpful と同義

□両親は彼を有名校にやるのにいろいろ犠牲を払いました ⇨ His parents made many sacrifices to send him to a prestige school.
　▶この表現では, sacrifice は通例複数形. 動詞表現：His parents sacrificed themselves to send him to a prestige school.

□彼は容易に環境に適応した ⇨ He found it easy to adjust (himself) to the environment.
　▶adjust (himself) to ～ は「～に適応する」意の熟語. adapt (oneself) to ～ も同義
　▶environment は, この意味では定冠詞 the を伴う

□その空港の近くに住んでいる人々は, ジェットの騒音のため, 昔の静かな生活を破壊されたと訴えている ⇨ The people living close to the airport complain that the noise of jet engines has destroyed their once placid way of life.

□ピートはいつもささいなことをうるさく言う ⇨ Pete always makes a noise about trifles.
　▶make a noise about ～ は「～についてうるさく不平を言う」の意の熟語. complain about ～ と同義

□座って静かになさい. 人の迷惑にならないようにね. ⇨ Sit down and be quiet! Don't make a nuisance of yourself.
　▶make a nuisance of oneself は, 「人の迷惑になる」の意の熟語

□騒音や煤煙(ばいえん)を出す工場は往々にして近所迷惑なものである ⇨ Noisy or smoky factories are often a nuisance to the neighborhood.

□私の家の近所は，非常に静かで，買物にも便利です ⇨ My house is in a very quiet neighborhood and also convenient for shopping.

□日本の東は太平洋に面している ⇨ Japan faces the Pacific on the east.
　▶この face は他動詞.「その建物は南に向いている」⇨ The building faces (to the) south.

□日本は海に囲まれた島国である ⇨ Japan is an island country surrounded by the sea.
　▶「囲まれている」状態をいう場合は, surrounded by が多く用いられる

□日本には火山と温泉地が多い ⇨ There are many volcanoes and hot springs in Japan.

□この地方には，見物に値する名所旧跡が多い ⇨ There are many scenic and historic spots worth seeing in this area.

□日本人は勤勉な国民だと言われている ⇨ The Japanese are said to be a hard-working people.

□日本語は外国人にはむずかしい言語である ⇨ Japanese is a difficult language for foreigners to learn.

□外国語を学ぶ最良の方法は何ですか ⇨ What is the best way to learn a foreign language?

□東京の人口はどれくらいか ⇨ What is the population of Tokyo?
　▶How large is the population of Tokyo? も同義. the population の後の前置詞は of が普通

第15章 社会・環境・国際事情

- 東京の人口は **1000万人以上である** ⇨ Tokyo has a population of more than 10 million.
  - ▶この population は，不定冠詞 a をつけて用いる
- 日本は，人口が稠密(ちゅうみつ)な国である ⇨ Japan is a densely [thickly] populated country.
  - ▶「人口希薄な地方」⇨ a sparsely [thinly] populated district
- その製薬工場から出る有害な廃棄物が近くの河川にたくさん流入していると，今日の新聞が報じている ⇨ Today's newspaper says that a lot of poisonous waste from the chemical works is going into the river nearby.
  - ▶waste は，「廃棄物」の意. works は factory (工場) の意
- 日本の勤労者の月平均所得 ⇨ the average monthly income of wage earners in Japan
- 父は **600万円の年収を得ています** ⇨ My father earns [makes, gets] an annual income of six million yen.
  - ▶「収入以上の暮らしをする」⇨ live beyond one's income /「収入以内で生活する」⇨ live within one's income
- 日本の主な農作物 ⇨ the principal farm produce in Japan
  - ▶farm produce [prɔ́djuːs] は「農産物」の意.「工場製品」は factory products という
- 自動車の月産台数 ⇨ the monthly production of automobiles
- 労使関係 ⇨ labor-management relations
- 貿易の黒字[赤字] ⇨ trade surplus [deficits]
- 日本の主な輸出先 ⇨ the principal markets for Japan
- 日本を研究している外国人 ⇨ a foreigner studying things Japanese

□国連は，世界平和・安全保障・協力を促進させる目的で形成された国際機関である ⇨ The United Nations is an international organization, formed to promote international peace, security and cooperation.

□日本は国連の一員として世界平和に貢献する責任がある ⇨ Japan has [bears] a responsibility for contributing to world peace as a member of the United Nations.
▶形容詞表現：Japan is responsible for contributing to world peace as a member of the United Nations.

Let's Try

【Ⅰ】 下の囲みの中に与えられている語群から最も適当な語を選択し，英文の空所に挿入し，文意を完成しなさい．

1. It is difficult to (　　) up a conversation with someone who only says 'Yes' and 'No.'
2. I have been trying all morning to get in (　　) with Mr. Jones.
3. When two women meet for the first time, they do not usually (　　) hands.
4. Henry is in (　　) of the office while his boss is away.
5. Mary and her sister (　　) turns helping their mother each night.

---
carry　　charge　　change　　keep　　shake
touch　　take

■[ヒント] 1. (　　) up＝continue「続ける」　2. get in (　　) with ～「～と連絡をとる」　3.「握手する」　4. in (　　) of ～＝responsible for ～「～を管理する」　5. (　　)

第15章　社会・環境・国際事情　　　　　233

turns「交替する」
■[解 答]　1. keep　2. touch　3. shake　4. charge　5. take

【II】　文尾の（　　）内の説明と等しい意味をもつ一語を，空所に挿入し，英文を完成しなさい．
　1. You are at (　　) to go wherever you like. (＝free)
　2. We have a good (　　) of his organizing ability. (＝think well of)
　3. I am not in (　　) of giving votes to young people of eighteen. (＝in sympathy with)
　4. His professional knowledge has been of great (　　) to us. (＝helpful, useful)
　5. If you want to finish this work by five o'clock, you should get (　　) to business right away. (＝begin to give serious attention to)

■[ヒント]　1.「好きなところに自由に行ってよい」　2.「彼の組織力を高く評価している」　3.「18歳の若者に選挙権を与えることに賛成できない」　4.「彼の専門知識はわれわれに非常に役に立った」　5.「5時までにこの仕事を完了したいなら，すぐ真剣に取りかかるべきだ」
■[解 答]　1. liberty　2. opinion　3. favor　4. service　5. down

【III】　日本文の意味になるように，英文の空所に適当な一語を補いなさい．
　1. Thank you very much (　　) all that you have done for me.
　　　（いろいろお世話になり，ありがとうございました）
　2. It was (　　) late for me to be sorry.

(後悔しても追いつかなかった)
3. It's pretty difficult to take time (   ).
   (なかなか休みが取れない)
4. I was a constant (   ) of anxiety for my parents since I was a sickly child.
   (私は病弱な子どもだったので、親には苦労の種でした)
5. It's a real problem when you can't (   ) in a foreign country.
   (外国で言葉が通じないと本当に困る)

■[ヒント] 1. thank＋目的語＋(前置詞)で「～に感謝する」の意. 2.「後悔先に立たず」の意. 3.「非番で」の意の副詞. cf.「1日休みを取る」take a day off 4.「もと, 源」の意. 5.「話が通じ合う」の意

■[解答] 1. for 2. too 3. off 4. source 5. communicate

Let's Memorize

1. 人間は環境に影響されやすいものだ.	People are easily influenced by their environment.
2. 子供たちには幸福な家庭環境が必要である.	Children need a happy home environment.
3. この道路建設は環境破壊の一因になっている.	This road construction is one factor in environmental disruption.
4. 彼は新しい環境に順応しようとしない.	He won't adapt himself to the new surroundings.
5. 彼はようやくこの国の暮らしに慣れてきた.	He has got used to life in this country.
6. 日本の物事のやり方が,	The Japanese way of doing

国際社会でいつも通用するとは限らない．

things is not always recognized by the international community.

7. だんだん女性の社会的進出がさかんになっている．

More and more women are taking an active part in social affairs.

8. 彼は公共のために自分の利益を犠牲にした．

He sacrificed his personal interest for the public good.

9. 先日は大変ご厄介になりました．

I'm sorry to have put you to so much trouble the other day.

10. たばこの煙で部屋の空気が汚れている．

The air in the room is filled with tobacco smoke.

11. 彼女は女手ひとつで苦労して5人の子供を育て上げた．

She worked as hard as she could to bring up five children all by herself.

12. その風景は言い尽くせないほど美しい．

The beauty of the scenery is beyond description.

13. 日本はまだ欧米から学ぶことが多い．

There is still quite a lot Japan can learn from Europe and America.

14. アメリカと比較して，日本は閉鎖社会だと思っている人が多い．

Many people think that Japan is a closed society compared with America.

15. 外国に住んでいると，故郷が懐かしいものだ．

When we live abroad, we sometimes miss home.

Exercises

〈例題 1〉

日本は長い間，世界から隔絶された閉鎖的な社会であった．しかし，近ごろは，多くの外国人が日本に住んでおり，そのため，他国人と逢ったり，彼らと考えを交換し合うことが一層容易となっている．それゆえ，大学時代に，ひとりだけでもよいから外国人の親しい友人を持ちなさいと，いいたい．

■[語句]「閉鎖的な社会」a closed society /「彼らと考えを交換する」exchange ideas with them /「大学時代」while you are in college, when you are a college student /「外国人の親しい友人」a good foreign friend

■[考え方]「世界から隔絶された閉鎖的な社会」は，「その他の世界から孤立した閉鎖的社会」と解し，a closed society isolated from the rest of the world と訳す．「そのため，他国人と逢ったり...交換し合うことが一層容易となっている」は，so it is easier for us to ～ の不定詞構文を用いる．最後の，「～を持ちなさいと，いいたい」は，I would like to suggest that you have ～ か，I advise you to try to have ～ などの勧誘の表現にする

〈解 答 例〉

(i) Japan has long been a closed society isolated from the rest of the world. These days, however, many foreign people are living in Japan, so it is easier for us to meet people from other countries and to exchange thoughts and ideas with them. I would like to suggest, therefore, that you have at least one good foreign friend while you are in college.

(ii) Japan has been a closed society, cut off from communication with the outside world, for a long time. These days, however, there are many foreign people living in Japan. This makes it easier for us to meet and share ideas with foreign people. For this reason I advise you to try to have at least one close foreign friend when you are a college student.

☆

──〈例題 2〉──
　日本では，サラリーマンは，遠隔の地，ときには外国へ転勤になることがある．そんなとき困ることのひとつは，子供の転校があまり容易でないということである．結局，家族を残して，新しい外国の土地で，ひとり暮らしを始める人が多い．

■[語 句]　「サラリーマン」office employees, office workers /「転校」change schools /「結局」eventually
■[考え方]　「転勤になる」は，「～に行くことを命ぜられる」か，transfer（転勤させる）を受動態にする．「困ることのひとつは，子供の転校があまり容易でないということである」は，「問題のひとつ」を主語にし，あとを that に導かれる名詞節にする．その名詞節内は，動名詞か，不定詞を用い，「子供が転校することが容易でない」と訳す．つまり，changing their children's school is no easy work [job] か，it is not so easy for their children to change schools.「結局，家族を残して．．．人が多い」は，「このため，彼らの多くのものが，しまいには家族を残して，ひとりで．．．住む」と考えて，This is why many of them often end up leaving their family at home to live alone ．．．または Eventually, many of them often leave their family behind, and go to live alone と訳す．「新しい外国の土地」は，「新しい任地」と解して，in the new place of one's appoint-

ment, または in the foreign country where they have to work とすると，一層具体的な表現となる

〈 解　答　例 〉

(i)　In Japan, office employees are often ordered to go to remote places or sometimes to foreign countries.　One of the problems confronting them is that changing their children's school is no easy work.　This is why many of them often end up leaving their family at home to live alone in the new place of their appointment.

(ii)　Office workers in Japan are often transferred to distant places or occasionally to foreign countries.　In such a case, one of the problems is that it is not so easy for their children to change schools.　Eventually, many of them often leave their family behind, and go to live alone in the foreign country where they have to work.

☆

―〈例題 3〉―
　青少年の健全な成長のためには，家庭の果たす役割が非常に大きな比重を占めている．親を中心に，家族全員が協力し合う家庭は，子どもの心に家族を思いやるやさしさを育てる．

■[語　句]　「青少年の健全な成長のため」promote [encourage] the sound growth of young people /「役割を果たす」play a part [a role] in /「～を思いやるやさしさを育てる」develop sympathetic concern for ～, have consideration for the feelings of ～

■[考え方]　「青少年の健全な成長のためには，家庭の果たす役割が非常に大きな比重を占めている」は，「家庭は青少年の健全な成長を促進するのに，重要な役割を果たす」と解し，play

第15章 社会・環境・国際事情

an important part in ～ing の頻出句を用いる．「親を中心に家族全員が協力し合う家庭」は，「家族全員が，親を中心にして，進んで互いに助け合うならば」と考え，If 節にするか，「親の指揮のもとに，家族全員が互いに協力し合う家庭では…」と解する

〈解 答 例〉

(i) Home plays an important part in encouraging the sound growth of young people. If all the family are willing to help each other, with the parents as the central figures, the children will have consideration for the feelings of their entire family.

(ii) A home environment plays an important role in promoting the wholesome growth of young people. In the home where all the family co-operate with each other under the leadership of the parents, the children can develop sympathetic concern for the rest of their family.

☆

―〈例題 4〉―
昔から日本人には島国根性があるとよく言われる．たしかに，そういう面もあるだろうが，見方を変えれば，日本人ほど外国語の好きな国民はまれだと思う．

■[語句]　「島国根性がある」insular, narrow-minded /「見方を変えれば」viewed from another angle

■[考え方]　「島国根性がある」は「島国根性がある国民である」と解し，現在完了時制を用いる．「そういう面もあるだろう」は，「これはいくぶん本当かも知れない」と訳す．「見方を変えれば」は，「日本を別の見方でみれば」と解する．「日本人ほど外国語の好きな国民はまれだ」は，「～ほど…なものはない」の比較構文で英訳する

〈解　答　例〉

(i)　It is often said that since olden times the Japanese have been an insular people. To be sure, this is partly true. Viewed from another angle, however, no peoples are as fond of foreign languages as the Japanese.

(ii)　It is often pointed out that since early times the Japanese have been a narrow-minded people. This may be partly true, but if we look at Japan from a different point of view, we may say that few peoples love foreign languages as ardently as the Japanese.

☆

─〈例題 5〉─
人類をはじめとする生物が，この地球上で生きていけるのは，大気，水，土の3つがそろっているからだ．どれが欠けても，どれが汚染されても，人間は生きていけない．

■[語　句]　「生物」creatures /「欠ける」missing, lacking /「汚染される」be polluted, become contaminated

■[考え方]　第1文は，「人間を含む，すべての生物が地球上に生存できる．なぜならば，3つのもの，空気，水，土が得られるからだ」と解する．第2文は，仮定法過去を用い，If＋動詞の過去形，帰結の主節は助動詞 could＋動詞の原形にする．または，未来に対する仮定を表わして，should を用いることもできる

〈解　答　例〉

(i)　All creatures, including human beings, can live on the earth, because three things are available, air, water and earth. If any one of them were missing or polluted, people could no longer survive.

第 15 章　社会・環境・国際事情　　　　　　　　　241

(ii) All animals, as well as humans, can live on this earth only because the three most vital elements, air, water and earth, are all present. People could not live, should any one of them be lacking or become contaminated.

INDEX
(Check & Check よりピックアップしました)

ア

愛嬌がある　211
挨拶状を出す　99
挨拶の仕方　99
愛社精神　218
愛情を抱く　214
愛読書　143
赤字を出さないようにする　49
あごひげを生やしている　99
朝寝坊する　96
頭が痛い　33
油絵　113
油絵を描く　114
雨やどりする　3
雨があがる　3
雨が多い　3
雨が降ったりやんだりする　2
雨が降りそうだ　2
雨がやんだ　3
雨が雪に変わる　4
危うく難を逃れる　128
暗記する　148

イ

家を借りる　21
家を建てる　21

生きがいを感じる　47
息が切れた　34
育成強化　165
(〜の)意見によると　149
意見を言う　149
医者にみてもらう　35
医者を開業している　37
医者を呼ぶ　35
衣食住　17
一日おきに　53
一日中　53
一生の友　47
1等賞を取る　117
いつものこと　96
いなか丸出しのなまりで話す　147
胃にもたれる　35
居眠りする　36
胃の具合が悪い　35
今ごろは　6
(〜が)いやになる　53
飲酒運転　132

ウ

宇宙時代　164
宇宙飛行士　164
宇宙旅行　65
雨天順延する　116
生まれがよい　46

[243]

海に囲まれている 230
(赤ん坊を)産む 228
(〜に)うるさい 18
(〜について)うるさく不平を言う 229
売れ行きがよい 198
運がいい[悪い] 214
運動会 116
運動する 115
運動不足 115

エ

英会話を習う 113, 146
(ストーリーを)映画化する 112
映画監督 112
映画俳優 112
映画評 112
映画を作る 112
映画を見に行く 112
(〜に)影響を及ぼす 161
栄枯盛衰 47
英語で授業を行なう 177
英語を使いこなす 147
駅弁 66
エネルギーの浪費 164
絵の才能がある 113

オ

(チームを)応援する 117
応急手当てをする 34
往復切符 66
応用科学 162
大当たりの 111
大雪 4
屋内競技 116

行ないを改める 216
怒りやすい 211
おごる 18, 100
お辞儀する 100
おしゃべりな人 147
お使いに行く 68
お年玉 100
思いやりがない 215
卸し商 196
恩給[年金]で暮らす 49, 199
温泉場[地] 8, 230
音痴である 113
温度が上がる[下がる] 8
温度の激変 8

カ

(国会が)開会中である 194
海外へ旅行する 65
開業医 35
外交官 195
外交関係を樹立する 195
外国語に熟達する 147
外国語を習い始める 147
外国文化を取り入れる 162
改札口 66
外食する 19
改造[築]する 22
解放される 227
課外活動に参加する 178
科学技術 162
化学の実験をする 165
書き誤り 148
学位を取る 181
各駅停車の列車 66
核戦争[兵器] 164
学費に困る 181

INDEX

火災報知器　130
火山　230
火事が起きる　130
火事が消しとめられる　130
餓死する　48, 130
(～が)火事で焼失する　130
貸し家　21
家事を(うまく)切り盛りする　21, 215
家事を手伝う　199
ガス爆発で破壊される　131
風邪がはやっている　32
風邪をひく　32
片道切符　66
活[休, 死]火山　130
楽器をひく　110
学校に出席する　182
学校の成績がいい[悪い]　177
合唱する　113
家庭生活　45
金をかけて～する　182
雷が落ちる　131
雷が鳴る　7
髪を長くしている　99
画廊　114
我を押し通す　217
(いい)考えを思いつく　216
環境汚染　133
観光[行楽]地　7, 65
観光の名所　65
感謝する　213
観衆　117
(他人の)感情を害する　149
間食をする　17
願書を提出する　181
感心する　212

キ

議案を提出する　195
気温が～度である　8
飢饉で苦しむ　131
気候　2, 5
寄港する　67
技術刷新　162
技術水準　162
気象衛星　163
犠牲を払う　229
季節はずれ　7
北風が吹く　7
切手収集　110
切手を貼る　81
切符売場　112
気に入る　217
(～を)気にかけている　149
厳しい冬　4
基本的人権　227
気むづかしい　47
着物を着る[脱ぐ]　19
客車　66
客をくつろがせる　98
救急車　131
救急所　131
急[慢]性病　37
教育制度　179
行儀が悪い　94
行儀作法にやかましい　211
競技者　116
競技種目　116
行儀の悪い子　211
供給　197
興味をもつ　110
霧が晴れる　7

記録映画　112
気を落とす　213
禁煙する　35
緊急着陸する　133
近所迷惑である　229
勤勉　212
勤労者所得　231

ク

クイズ番組　114
薬が効いた　36
薬を飲む　35
癖がつく　94
癖で　99
(悪い)癖をやめる　95
靴がきつい　20
暮らし向きがよい[悪い]　199
クラス会を開く　98
来る日も来る日も　53
車で出勤する　62

ケ

経験で学ぶ　148
経済事情　197
経済状態を向上させる　197
芸術品　114
景勝の地　65
外科医　35
劇を上演する　112
景色を見渡す　178
下宿暮らしをする　22
結婚する　48
傑作　143
決勝戦で勝つ[負ける]　117
仮病を使う　36

下痢する　35
言外の意味を読む　143
研究に専念する　162
健康診断を受ける　32
健康である　31
健康に注意する　31
健康を害する　32
健康を増進する　32
検札にくる　66
原子物理学[者]　163
原子力時代　164
原子力潜水艦　164
原子力発電所　164
原子力を利用する　164
建設中　22
現代社会　226
見当がつかない　216
見物に値する　230
権利を尊重する　227
権利を保護する　227
言論の自由　227

コ

後悔する　216
高架を走る列車　69
高給をとる　49
公共心のある　218
工業先進国　161
公共輸送機関　68
航空便で　81
口語で　147
(～を)行使する　227
公衆道徳に欠ける　218
工場製品　231
洪水地　131
洪水で大損害を受ける　129

INDEX

(〜を)後世に伝える　160
高層建築地域　22
高速道路　68
高速度で走る　66
交通が途絶する　63
交通事故　127
交通事故が起きる　128
交通渋滞　63
交通の混雑を緩和する　63
交通量が多い　62
交通を整理する　63
好天に恵まれる　1
校内暴力　182
鉱物資源に富む　163
紅葉する　8
紅葉の名所　8
行楽地　65
小売商　196
考慮に入れる　215
高齢である　48
高齢で死ぬ　48
語学　147
語学が達者である［弱い］　147
語学を修得する　147
国技　117
国際機関　232
国際競技　116
国際語　150
国産品　196
国内生産　198
国宝　161
国連　232
国連加盟　195
国連加盟国　195
固執する　217
個人教授を受ける　182
国会　194

国会議員に立候補する　193
小包みで　81
言葉が通じない　150
言葉を聞き覚える　146
こぬか雨　3
好みに合って　111
根気　212
混んでいる　63
困難に打ち勝つ　213
婚約している　48

サ

災害地　127
財産を築く　212
菜食主義　18
咲いている　5
策を講じる　195
酒に強い　19
ささいなこと　229
刺身　18
寒さにふるえる　8
参考書　146

シ

試合に勝つ［負ける］　117
自衛権　227
時間がかかる　50
時間切れである　54
時間通りに　50
時間に追われる　53
時間に正確である　52
時間の観念がない　53
時間の許す限り　53
時間をさく　53
時間をつぶす　50

資金をつぎ込む 198
試験がある 177
試験でカンニングする 181
試験に首尾よく合格する 177
試験に落第する 177
資源を愛護する 164
自己紹介する 81
事故にあう 128
視察旅行 65
時差ボケ 67
死傷者 133
辞職する 199
地震がある 129
地震が多い 129
地震に耐えられる 129
地震に弱い 129
地震を予知する 129
自炊する 17
自然科学 162
自然現象 162
自然食をとる 18
自然の法則 162
試着する 19
歯痛 33
(大量の)失業者が出る 165
失業する 198
失言する 148
実社会に出る 228
湿度が高い 6
実用放送衛星 163
しとしとと雨が降る 3
辞任する 193
私費で 182
辞表を提出する 199
自分の考えを表現する 149
(〜で)死亡する 37
島国 230

自慢する 215
霜がおりる 8
謝意を表する 213
(よい)社会人となる 226
社会の風習に従う 226
社会問題 133
車掌 66
写真の映りがいい 113
写真を現像[焼きつけ]する 113
写真を撮る 113
写真を引き伸ばす 113
社説 144
借金している 47
自由 227
修学旅行 65
自由を奪う 227
習慣が異なる 95
(悪い)習慣がつく 95
習慣に従う 95
習慣になじむ 99
(良い)習慣をつける 94
充実した生活を送る 47
(〜に)従順である 212
就職口をさがす 198
就職を申し込む 198
終身雇用制 199
重態である 33
住宅不足 22
収入以上の生活をする 47, 231
収入内で生活する 47, 231
就任する 193
重要文化財 161
〜主演の映画 111
授業がある 179
授業が始まる 179
授業をさぼる 179
授業を休む 179

INDEX

(〜の)主義を貫く 217
祝日 100
祝辞を述べる 98
宿題をやる 178
手術を受ける 34
手術をする 34
出勤する 193
出港する 67
出版される 145
出版の自由 227
出費を惜しまない 197
趣味が良い 111
趣味と実益に 112
趣味をもつ 110
需要 197
需要を満たす 198
旬である 7
上映中の 111
省エネする 164
消火器 130
奨学金をもらう 180
消化によい 19
正気づく 217
昇給する 49
焼死する 48, 130
招待される 80
招待を受ける 81
招待を断る 80
上天気 1
商売をする 196
消防車 131
食が進む 19
食事の作法 18
食事の仕度をする 17
食餌療法を始める 18
食事を片づける 17
食事をする 17

食卓につく 18
食堂車 66
職につく 198
食糧不足 19
初秋 8
初春に 5
新学期 179
真剣に努力する 213
人口が稠密である 231
人口希薄な 231
深刻な水不足 5
辛酸をなめる 47
(家が)浸水する 131
人生観 45
人生のはかなさ 215
心臓専門医 35
寝台車 66
新築の家 21
審判 117
新聞が〜と報じている 231
新聞で〜を知る 144
新聞の見出しになる 144
新聞を購読する 14
進歩する 161

ス

水彩画 113
睡眠不足 36
水路で旅行する 65
すぐに〜する 51
すし詰めで 63
すたれている 97
ストをする 197
スピードを上げる 66
ずぶぬれ 2
〜することにしている 97

〜するのに苦労する 51

セ

晴雨にかかわらず 2
政界に入る 193
政界の事情に通じている 194
生化学[者] 163
生活が楽である 46
生活水準を向上させる 45
生活に困っている 46
(〜の)生活に適応する 51
生計をたてる 45
生産高 231
正々堂々とやる 117
政党 194
成年に達する 48
西洋文明を輸入する 161
清廉潔白な人 211
世界一周の旅行をする 65
世界新記録をたてる 117
世界平和に貢献する 195, 232
責任がある 232
責任感が強い 210
席をゆずる 66
絶版である 145
せりふを暗記する 114
世論 228
善悪を区別する 210
全員出席 182
専攻する 150, 181
戦災者 127
先日 53
先週の今日 53
先進国 161
選択科目 177
前途有望である 217

ソ

騒音公害 133
葬式が行なわれる 48
速達で 81
速読する 143
ソバを食べる 100
空模様が怪しい 2
(この)空模様では 3

タ

退院する 34
大学教育を受ける 176
退学する 180
大学生活を楽しむ 182
大学に進学する 178
大学に入学を許可される 178
(子供を)大学にやる 182
大学入試を受ける 177
大気汚染 133
大惨事を招く 127
大使館 194
(駐米)大使に任じられる 194
退職する 49, 199
体調を保つ 31
体調を整える 31
台風が接近している 7
台風が被害を与える 129
台風の季節 7
ダイヤが乱れる 128
(〜のところに)立ち寄る 83
多読する 143
他人の陰口を言う 211
他人の気持ち 215
他人の苦しみ 215

楽しみにしている 215
だまっている 148
タラップを上がる[おりる] 67
探検旅行 65
炭鉱の爆発 131
誕生日を祝う 98
団体旅行をする 66
団地 21

チ

近いうちに 53
近い将来に 53
近頃 53
地下鉄に乗る 69
地球物理学[者] 163
着陸する 64
忠告に従う 212
長寿の秘訣 34
聴力を失う 33
治療を受ける 34
賃上げ要求する 197
賃金 197

ツ

ついている(運がいい) 214
(電車などで)通勤する 62
通信衛星 163
つき合いにくい 47
つき合っている 78
尽くす 228
津波がおそう 131
梅雨が明けた 6
梅雨にはいった 6
つりに行く 115

テ

停電 128
手紙の返事をする 79
手紙を書く 79
手紙を出す 81
でき合いを買う 20
(〜に)適応する 229
適度の運動 115
鉄道が不通になる 128
鉄道事故 127
鉄道で旅行する 65
徹夜マージャンをする 112
テレビ娯楽番組 114
テレビ視聴者 114
テレビの時報 50
テレビのスター 114
テレビ番組 114
テレビをつける[消す] 114
テレビを見る 114
天気が変わりやすい 1
天気がぐずつく 2
電気が伝わる 165
天気が続く 2
天気がよければ 2
天気予報によれば 2
電気を起こす 165
天災 127
電車で通学する 62
伝染病 37
電卓 165
転地する 33
伝導体 163
天然資源を開発する 163
電報を受け取る 81
電報を打つ 81

電話する　83
電話中　82
電話ですます　83
電話で長話しをする　146
電話で話す　83
電話に出る　82
電話を借りる　82
電話を切らないでおく　82
電話を切る　82
電話を引く　23

ト

倒産する　197
凍死する　48, 130
同情する　214
統率力　227
登頂する　115
投票権がある　227
独自の文明　162
読書好き　143
徳の高い人　212
時計が(〜時を)打つ　50
時計が狂っている　50
時計が(〜時を)指す　50
時計が(〜秒)進む[遅れる]　49
ところによってにわか雨　3
年相応に振舞う　47
年相応に見える　47
どしゃ降り　2
年より若くみえる　46
年をとるにつれて　215
特急　66
隣に住む　23
隣の人　23
とばし読みする　143
徒歩で通学する　62

徒歩旅行　65
トランプで運を占う　112
トランプをする　112
取引をする　196

ナ

内科医　35
長生きする　34
名を汚す　180

ニ

似合う　20
憎む　214
日曜画家　113
日曜大工　113
日本風　21
入院[退院]する　34
入学願書　181
入学志願者　181
入学試験の準備を始める　177
入港する　67
入試に失敗する　213
入場禁止　112
入場無料　112
入場料　112
にわか雨　2

ネ

熱が出る　33
熱[胃]の薬　35
熱を計る　34
年賀状を出す　99
年功序列制　199
年収　231

INDEX

ノ

農作物　231
濃霧　6
のどが痛い　33
(電車に)乗り遅れる　51, 62
乗り心地がよい　65
乗り越す　63

ハ

廃棄物　231
ハイキングに行く　115
舶来品　196
箸を使う　100
罰金を科せられる　132
(新聞の)発行部数　145
発展途上国　161
初詣でする　100
派手好き　20
(人に)話しかける　149
(電話が)話し中　82
早合点する　217
はやっている　97
早寝早起きする　96
はやりだ　97
春のきざし　5
春めく　5
晴れ着　20
晴れそうだ　2
晴れた日　1
(タイヤが)パンクする　132
万歳を三唱する　117
晩餐会を催す　98
晩秋　8
繁盛する　195

半導体　163
(川が)氾濫する　131

ヒ

日当たりがいい　22
ピアノの伴奏で歌う　113
ピアノを教える　113
日帰り旅行　64
日が長い　6
避寒地　7
(〜を)低く見る　228
飛行機に乗り込む[から降りる]　67
日ごとに暖かくなる　5
久しく雨がない　3
久しぶりに　54
美術館　114
美術展覧会　114
非常出口　131
避暑地　7
引っ越す　22
必修科目　177
日照り続き　3
日増しに　53
(高く)評価している　227
病気が快方に向かう　32
病気が軽い[重い]　37
病気が治る　32
病気になる　37
病人　36
評判がいい　46
費用を切り詰める　197
昼寝する　36

フ

風俗・習慣　94

深く読む 143
不況に見舞われる 196
福祉を増進する 226
服装 99
腹痛 33
不健康である 31
不作 8
不作法 216
不時着する 67
普段着 20
物価が上[下]がっている 196
物価が高い 45
物価に対する政策 228
筆無精 80
不動産売買業者 196
太る 34
踏切 128
古本で買う 145
古本屋 145
文化遺産 160
文化が進む 161
文化活動 160
文化勲章を受ける 162
文化交流 160
文化祭を行なう 161
文化施設 161
文化人 160
文化水準を高める 160
噴火する 130
文化的国民 160
文化の水準が高い 228
文化の進んだ国[民] 160
文化の高い[低い]国 160
文化をはかる尺度 228
文庫本 144
分譲マンション 21
文人 144

文通する 80
(〜する)分別がある 210
文明の進歩 161

ヘ

平均寿命 34
平和国家 195
ベッドタウンに住む 22
部屋を予約する 65
ベルトをしめる[はずす] 67
勉強を怠ける 177
(〜に対して)偏見を持つ 212
返事を待つ 79
(〜に)便利である 230

ホ

法案を可決[通過]する 195
暴飲暴食する 19
貿易の黒字[赤字] 231
貿易摩擦 198
邦楽 115
豊作 8
放射能で汚染される 133
放送局 114
放送する 114
訪問する 83
募金する 199
母国語 148
ほめる 214
本心を打ち明ける 148
本に夢中である 144
翻訳で読む 146
本を隅から隅まで読む 144
本を精読する 143
本を手当たり次第に読む 143

INDEX

マ

まさかの時　199
間違いを恐れる　149
真夏に　4
(列車に)間に合う　62
真冬に　4
満開である　6
漫画本　146
慢性病　37
満足する　214
満点をとる　177

ミ

南向き　22
見舞いに行く　35
耳が遠い　33
(～に)身を入れる　182
民間放送　114

ム

昔からの習慣　95
無口な人　147
蒸し暑い　6
(～に)夢中である　113
(～に)無とんちゃくである　215

メ

名所旧跡　65, 230
迷信に左右される　165
名誉となる　180
(人の)迷惑になる　229
(～に)面している[向いている]　230

モ

喪があける　48
木造家屋　21
目的を達成する　213
喪に服する　48
模倣で学ぶ　148

ヤ

野外競技　116
約束する　213
約束の時間に遅れる　51
約束を守る[破る]　213
(～の)役に立つ　228
(～の)役を演じる　111
やせる　34
野党　194
山の天気　1
山登りに行く　115
やりくりする　45

ユ

有害な　231
(～する)勇気がある　210
優勝する　116
優等で卒業する　180
郵便料　81
雪合戦をする　9
雪が積っている　8
雪が解ける　5
(よく)雪が降る　4
雪国　9
雪ダルマを作る　9
(列車が)雪に弱い　130

雪道　8

ヨ

良い点をとる　177
用心する　218
洋風　21
予算をたてる　49
予習をする　177
与党　194
夜ふかしする　96, 145
(～に)よろしく　84

ラ

来客がある　78
来週の今日　53
落胆する　213
酪農に従事する　197
ラジオ講座　114
ラジオの音を小さくする[大きくする]　114
ラジオをつける[消す]　114

リ

利益を得る　197
陸の旅行　64
陸路で旅行する　65
罹災者　127
理想を実現する　218
立身出世する　228
流行を追う　97
療法　36

旅行案内業者　64
旅行者用小切手　68
旅行代理店　64
旅行をする　63, 65
離陸する　64

レ

礼儀正しい　211
礼儀を知らない　211
冷暖房してある～　22
列車が脱線，転覆する　129
列車から降りる　62
列車と衝突する　128
列車に乗る　62
列車を乗り換える　66
列車をまちがえる　66
連絡がない　80
連絡する　80

ロ

労使関係　231
漏電　130

ワ

若葉が萌え始める　5
話題が豊富である　148
わびる　216
和服　20
割り勘　100
われを忘れている　218

About the Authors

●小林兼之（こばやし　かねゆき）
　1922 年生まれ．青山学院大学英文科卒．51 年から 52 年にかけ，米国イリノイ大学大学院に留学．50 年より 80 年まで，東京都立板橋，白鷗，戸山高等学校の英語科主任を歴任．その間，全英連テスト部役員，青山学院大学講師を務める．69 年より代々木ゼミナール講師となり，外国人とのコンビで英作文を指導，その熱意とユーモアあふれる授業は，生徒達の人気を博し，現在に至る．

●Gary Hunt（ガリー・ハント）
　1951 年英国ウェールズに生まれる．ウェールズ大学スウォンジー校哲学科卒業（B.A.）後，ケンブリッジ大学において，Post Graduate Certificate of Education（教員課程）を修了．英国では，公立中学及び高校で，英文学を教えていた経験がある．1979 年に来日し，滞日 10 年を越える．現在は，代々木ゼミナール，明治大学において，英語の講師を務めている．

すぐ使える　英文ライティングのエッセンス

2004 年 9 月 8 日　初版発行
2010 年 4 月 30 日　3 刷発行

著　者　小　林　兼　之
　　　　ガリー・ハント
発行者　関　戸　雅　男
印刷所　研究社印刷株式会社

KENKYUSHA
〈検印省略〉

発行所　株式会社　研　究　社

〒 102-8152
東京都千代田区富士見 2-11-3
電話（編集）03 (3288) 7711 (代)
　　（営業）03 (3288) 7777 (代)
振替　00150-9-26710

ISBN 978-4-327-45181-3　C1082

装丁　吉崎克美